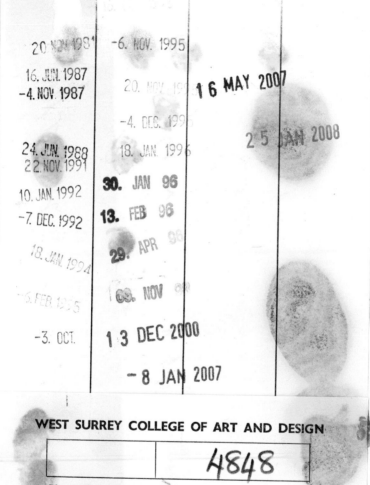

In Defence of Freedom

In Defence of Freedom

Edited by Dr K. W. Watkins

Essays by

Winston S. Churchill MP
Lord De L'Isle
Professor Antony Flew
John Gouriet
Dr Stephen Haseler
Russell Lewis
Norris McWhirter
Lady Morrison of Lambeth
Robert Moss
Narindar Saroop
Dr K. W. Watkins

Cassell
London

CASSELL & CO. LTD.
35 Red Lion Square, London WC1R 4SG
and at Sydney, Auckland, Toronto, Johannesburg,
an affiliate of
Macmillan Publishing Co., Inc.,
New York.

First published 1978

ISBN 0 304 29963 4

Photoset, printed and bound
in Great Britain by
REDWOOD BURN LIMITED
Trowbridge & Esher

Contents

Preface

In the last quarter of the twentieth century one great question confronts every man and woman in Britain. It is, in what sort of society do you wish your children and grandchildren to live? Historians of the future, when writing of Britain, will be intrigued not so much by the rise and fall of a great empire or even by her contribution to culture and science as by the freedom of her political institutions and the toleration they safeguarded. Their preservation today depends on the solution of the economic, moral and political problems that beset her. The authors of these essays, of different political parties and of none, offer these essays in the hope that they may make a contribution, however modest, to the Defence of Freedom.

K. W. Watkins
Sheffield, September 1977.

Lord De L'Isle

Freedom and the Constitution

This is a book about freedom by several hands. Each of the essays which follows offers a view upon a particular aspect of this theme.

To endure, freedom has to inspire a people with a moral discipline which allows them to entertain their own reasoned convictions and aims, and at the same time to be aware of the value of differing opinions and objectives and of the right of others to fulfil these within a plural society.

Equally, there must be a widespread realization that, though freedom has few avowed opponents—being generally held to be a virtuous idea—it has a number of adversaries, often in disguise. However, such enemies are less numerous than the friends who profess to support it but do not wish to acknowledge that the defence of freedom is an active duty. For, lacking firm conviction, they are loath to admit the truth that the conflict between libertarian and collectivist ideals cannot remain unresolved for very long within one polity, since these are directed to incompatible and mutually destructive ends.

Freedom is not merely an ideal to be proclaimed. For its preservation in practice it has to depend upon a firm, well joined structure, strong enough to withstand all the buffetings to which human institutions must be continuously exposed.

This essay sets out to consider in perspective the constitutional basis of a free and plural society in the United Kingdom.

In the administration of the law a connected system has been developed here over the centuries. The earliest legal commentaries were written in the thirteenth century and the famous Year Books also began during the same century.

But, notably, the theory of the British Constitution lacks the precision of an established discipline. As a nation we have hitherto fought shy of any clear definition of what is or is not a constitutional question. We have, in our optimistic way, left so far undefined the means to offer connected and codified solutions to the many constitutional and legal problems which today crowd upon us.

What are to be the relations of the Constitution and of our legal system to the structure and law of the European Community? Whether, and if so how, to devolve power to Scotland, Wales and Northern Ireland; how to maintain the unity and the universality of law, now gravely threatened: and how to re-balance Parliament, grossly over-weighted on the side of Government, supported by its majority in the Commons?

Our country has devoted more careful thought to promoting written Constitutions for former dependencies, become newly emergent nations, than any other power in history. The theory and practice of the division of powers between the legislative, executive and judicial arms of the State has over and over again been recognized. So has the need to prescribe their relations within a written document. This has to be constructed so as to leave open the means of changing its form and content by orderly, pre-determined steps to safeguard the Constitution, for the first time explicitly defined, from the abuse of authority by Government, designed to enjoy only a temporary lease of power.[1]

If we are candid, we must admit that there is a certain self-satisfaction in our national attitude. England, we feel, as the Mother of Parliaments, can do without the tiresome legalisms which less well-founded, more parvenu, systems have to suffer. Our good sense, our pragmatism, our tolerance, our mutually observed conventions, our inter-party contacts, our acknowledgement that the Parliamentary opposition is Her Majesty's Opposition, all combine to make us feel ourselves a peculiar people, eternally proof against the political dangers threatening lesser breeds having inferior traditions of democratic government.

Yet if we can free ourselves from deep-seated prejudices, if we have the detachment to stand back and look anew at the present state of the nation, we shall grasp that we require today far more urgently than ever before a frame of reference for the solutions which will have to be devised to meet our urgent constitutional dilemmas.

Lord Scarman[2] has said:

The common law has in theory no gaps or omissions, only a few silences which at any time upon the instigation of a litigant the voice of a judge can break.

And he has added:

The modern English judge still sees enacted law as an exception to, a graft upon, or a correction of the customary law in his hands; he gives unswerving loyalty to the enacted word of Parliament, but he construes that word strictly in its statutory context and always upon the premise, usually unspoken, that Parliament legislates against the background of an all-embracing customary law.

And this, later in the same series of lectures:

The system would not have survived until now had it not possessed great strength. First its independence, created and cherished by judges, owing nothing in its origin to Parliament, claiming to be customary law, it has an inbuilt resistance to the power of others, whether they be Barons or Trade Unions, Kings or Government Departments or even to Parliament itself. Its very existence is therefore a bulwark against oppression and tyranny, no matter who be the oppressor or tyrant.

It was indeed the strength of the common law, combined with the independence of Parliament which proved the bulwark against the pretensions to unfettered power of the first two Stuart Kings.

With the final submission of the Sovereign to the constitutional power of the Courts and of Parliament which was signalled by the accession of William and Mary to the English throne, the immediate threat to our liberties, which might have

resulted from a successful claim to prerogative power by James
II, was removed. Instead, the sovereignty of the King in Parliament was established as the supreme authority, first in England
and then in the United Kingdom.

It suited the ascendant Whig oligarchy to maintain the independence of the courts and thereby to support the common law.
But gradually the supremacy of Parliament has been narrowed
down to the supremacy of the House of Commons, the Chamber
which has become more and more subservient to successive
Ministries armed with ever-widened powers.

Parallel with this process there has been a progressive sapping
of the moral authority of the common law, and this in turn has
led to the erosion of the foundations of our unwritten Constitution, respect for law and for individual rights.

A good deal of the responsibility for emphasizing the unchallengeable authority of central government must be laid at the
door of nineteenth-century writers on the Constitution. This is
how the eminent constitutional lawyer, Dicey, puts his views:

England has, at any rate since the Norman Conquest, always been
governed by an absolute legislative authority, and the legislative authority of the Crown has never been curtailed, but has been transferred
from the Crown acting alone (or rather in Council) to the Crown
acting first with and then in subordination to the Houses of Parliament.[3]

At the beginning of his *Law of the Constitution* the author
professes that:

his duty is neither to attack nor to defend the Constitution, but simply
to explain the law.

But in the course of his work the optimistic outlook of a rather
insular Victorian much colours his conclusions. This is most
plainly seen when he is examining the Constitutions of other
countries and especially that of the United States. Here is an
example:

The difficulty of altering the Constitution (of the U.S.) produces conservative sentiment, and natural conservatism doubles the difficulty of
altering the Constitution. The House of Lords has lasted for centuries:

the American Senate has now existed for more than one hundred years, yet to abolish or alter the House of Lords might turn out to be an easier matter than to modify the Constitution of the Senate. . . . A federal Constitution always lays down general principles which from being placed in the Constitution gradually come to command a superstitious reverence. . . .

Dicey seems to have recognized the extreme implications of his assertion of the absolute power resident in Parliament. So to this 'first feature', as he calls it, 'the undisputed supremacy throughout the country of the central government', he adds a second, 'the supremacy of law', which he describes as 'the security given under the English Constitution to the rights of individuals'.

Among the various aspects of the Rule of Law, as Dicey describes them, is 'equality before the law' or 'the equal subjection of all classes to the ordinary law of the land administered by the ordinary Law Courts'.

He ends thus:

. . . the English Constitution is still marked far more deeply than is generally supposed by peculiar features. . . . These peculiar features may be summed up in the combination of Parliamentary sovereignty with the Rule of Law.

This comfortable doctrine allowed Dicey to write:

. . . that which the majority of the House of Commons demands, the majority of the English people usually desire.

However, Dicey prefaces the last and eighth edition of his great work, published in 1914, with a new Introduction, although the text remains unaltered. In this he reviews the changes in the Constitution over the preceding thirty years. He writes of some disturbing developments, of the 'new doctrine of lawlessness', of the consequences of the Parliament Act, 1911, which increased the power of party, and of the passing of the Trades Disputes Act, 1906, the fourth section of which he describes as 'the triumph of legalised wrong-doing'.

The extent to which our author reversed his earlier opinions is best shown in the concluding paragraphs of his Introduction:

The sovereignty of Parliament is still the fundamental doctrine of English constitutionalists. But the authority of the House of Lords has been gravely diminished, whilst the authority of the House of Commons, or rather the majority thereof during any one Parliament, has been immensely increased. Now that increased portion of sovereignty can be effectively exercised only by the Cabinet which holds in its hands the guidance of the party machine. And of the party which the parliamentary majority supports, the Premier becomes at once the legal head, and if he is a man of ability the real leader.

The result of a state of things which is not yet fully recognised inside or outside Parliament is that the Cabinet, under a leader who has studied and mastered the art of modern parliamentary warfare, can defy on matters of the highest importance the possible or certain will of the nation.

Dicey's assured earlier views thus appear in sharp contrast to his later doubts about the direction in which the English Constitution was being moved.

But the doctrine of parliamentary sovereignty, which his learning and literary gifts helped to promote, has established such deep roots in the soil of our politics that it has been able through vigorous assertion, to suppress, at least for practical purposes, that 'second feature' of the Constitution, 'the security given . . . to the rights of individuals', which has for more than two centuries reconciled the supremacy of Parliament to English libertarians.

For an up-to-date illustration of the effect on modern jurisprudence of the drift of opinion which Dicey foresaw in his latter days, let us consider the case of the Attorney-General *v.* Gouriet. This was settled in the House of Lords on 26 July 1977.[4]

In the preceding January Mr Gouriet had applied to the Attorney-General (Mr Silkin) for his *fiat* to allow him to take proceedings in the High Court to restrain the Union of Post Office Workers from implementing a threatened boycott of the mail to and from South Africa, acting as a private citizen asserting a public right. There was at no time any dispute that such a boycott would have been a criminal breach of a Statute in force. The Attorney-General refused his *fiat* to allow the plaintiff to proceed in a relator action in his name. Next, Mr Gouriet applied to a Judge in Chambers for leave to bring his suit. Again he was refused. So he applied to the Court of Appeal which granted him an immediate interim injunction, and this proved effective in stopping the boycott.

After hearings the following week, the Court of Appeal decided that it had jurisdiction to grant the plaintiff relief by a declaration which recited the actual words of the relevant sections of the governing Statute. The right of the Attorney-General to refuse his *fiat* had never been tested in the courts. Nor had the assertion that he was responsible to Parliament alone in all questions respecting his prerogative and so could bar access to the courts in all matters of public right.

It was common ground at the hearings in both courts that if Mr Gouriet had pursued the Post Office Union as a private citizen with a personal interest in preventing the proposed boycott, the courts could not have entertained the case. His action would have been in tort. The Trade Unions and Labour Relations Act 1974 has given trade unions complete protection against actions in tort. Thus the Attorney-General's claim to enjoy an unchallengeable prerogative in all circumstances to allow or not to allow a private citizen to bring an action in the public interest to prevent the committal of a criminal act would, if upheld, give a trade union complete immunity from any preventive judicial procedures in any case where the Attorney-General refused his *fiat*.

On appeal the House of Lords reversed the decision of the Court of Appeal. It struck out Mr Gouriet's application, awarding costs against him.

What the House of Lords decides is law. But the decision and the consequences which flow therefrom are of great future significance.

Commenting on the case as a former Attorney-General, Lord Shawcross has written:

The theory that the Attorney-General is answerable to Parliament may have been true enough in the days of Dicey. . . .[5]

He proceeds later:

The fact is that we have moved away from Dicey's age of reasoned democracy into the age of power. Responsibility to Parliament means

in practice at the most responsibility to the party commanding the
majority there which is the party to which the Attorney-General of the
day must belong. One has only to remember the so-called Shrewsbury
'Martyrs' and the Clay Cross affair to realise that the party will obviously not criticise the Attorney-General of the day for not taking
action which, if taken, might cause embarrassment to their political
supporters.

He adds:

. . . it requires no stretch of the imagination to assume that at some
future date we might have a majority in Parliament of extreme left or
extreme right persuasion with an Attorney-General of similar view.

Lord Shawcross goes on:

It is naive to observe, as was done in the Gouriet case,[6] that the
Attorney-General may have regard to political considerations but 'not
of course acting for party political reasons'. It is 'of course' exactly the
present appearance and the future possibility that he might so act
which endangers both existing respect for and the future effectiveness
of the rule of law. . . .

The Court of Appeal in granting Mr Gouriet relief had taken
its stand on the principle to which Lord Denning gave expression. He said, repeating a previous judgment in McWhirter
v. IBA:

If there is good cause for supposing that a Government Department or
a Public Authority (and I should add a trade union) is transgressing
the law, or is about to transgress it in a way which offends . . . . thousands of Her Majesty's subjects, then in the last resort any of those
offended . . . can draw it to the attention of the court and seek leave to
have the law enforced.[7]

Lord Lawton, in concurring, made the following pro-
nouncement:

I cannot and do not accept that he (the Attorney-General) and he
alone in relation to law enforcement in the Civil Courts is the sole arbi-
ter of what is in the public interest.

The House of Lords in reaching its unanimous decision
appears to have proceeded on precisely opposite legal and constitutional principles.

Under the heading 'The Public Interest', the *New Law Journal*[8] has sharply criticized its decision as 'reactionary'. The article has given particular consideration to Lord Wilberforce's judgment.

Lord Wilberforce stated:

That it is the exclusive right of the Attorney-General to represent the public interest even when individuals might be interested in a larger view of the matter is not technical, not procedural, not fictional. It is constitutional. I agree with Lord Westbury that it is also wise.

He went on:

The decisions to be taken in the public interest are not such as courts are fitted or equipped to make. The very fact that, as the present case very well shows, decisions are of the type to attract political criticism and controversy, shows that they are outside the range of discretionary problems which the courts can resolve.[9]

To these opinions the *New Law Journal* responds as follows:

We cannot with respect agree that the absolute exclusivity of the Attorney-General's power of intervention (including the power not to intervene and thereby to exclude the operation of the judicial process altogether) is 'wise'. Indeed, what was wise over 100 years ago is unlikely to be wise in the very different circumstances of today. Lord Wilberforce's statement that the Attorney-General enjoyed 'this exclusive right in order that he, and he alone, might represent the public interest' raises the question of what is the public interest. . . . His answer to it appears to proceed from the highly questionable premise that the Attorney-General alone is capable of deciding what the public interest is.

The article proceeds:

Many . . . will regret his [Lord Wilberforce's] suggestion that 'the very fact that decisions attract political criticism and controversy shows that they are outside the range of [those] which the courts [should take]', not least because he went on to say that this fact had been demonstrated 'very well' in the Gouriet case. How can the courts be said to be 'above politics' if they stand aloof for fear that an intervention by them might lead to 'political criticism' or 'controversy'. . . . To make the avoidance of that outcome an end in itself . . . is to play into the hands of those who would like to see the influence of the courts in 'public interest' matters reduced to a minimum.

In the course of his Hamlyn Lectures Lord Scarman very pertinently inquires 'The law is being remaindered—but to what?'

The decision in Attorney-General *v.* Gouriet should warn us that the law is being moved, and moved very fast, away from the principle of the security which it gives to the rights of individuals. We should mark Lord Scarman's warning:

When times are abnormally alive with fear and prejudice the common law is at a disadvantage; it cannot resist the will, however frightened and prejudiced of Parliament.

It is in such times that we can most clearly perceive the price we are paying for the absence of enforceable constitutional guarantees of human rights and of prohibitions restraining the power of Government.

Circumstanced as we are, we can foresee the effect of an announcement from the Judges' Bench that the law must take care to eschew any possibility of involvement in the political arena, however this may affect the rights of citizens.

Recent history tells us that it is the rule of law, as it is understood among free societies, which comes first under attack from parties 'of extreme left or extreme right persuasion'.

Indeed, though totalitarian regimes have come to power by various means—by revolution, by war or by conquest, they have also been achieved by an abuse of the democratic process and a subversion of an independent judicial system, including intimidation of judges.

As a result of World War II Western Germany is now a parliamentary democracy. Nevertheless, Hitler's rise to power between the wars is the most instructive example in modern history of the use of the ballot box to gain absolute authority in the State. To those who point justifiably to the force and fraud he used in his progress to dictatorship, it must be replied that any democracy which has first been weakened by the deliberate corruption of free institutions is ripe for a 'take-over', be it in the name of one leader or on behalf of a highly disciplined group capable of organizing mass support on a single-party basis.

Perhaps because they were closer in time to the eighteenth-century notion of autocracy as it prevailed in Europe, the Founding Fathers of the United States of America were anxious to safeguard the future of the infant Republic from the very outset against the dangers of concentrated power by incorporating in their Constitution a division of authority between the legislature, the executive and the judiciary. They were aware too, as students of the classics, that tyranny is based on popular acclaim. They gave explicit expression to the concept of limited sovereignty which was first developed under the English Common Law.

It can be said that the Constitution of the United States gave institutional expression to common law notions of freedom under the law. Hence the trouble taken to write into the Constitution articles which gave specific protection to private rights from encroachment either by the States or by the Federal Government.

The device which they employed was the vesting of an ultimate right for aggrieved parties to appeal to the Supreme Court against any enactment which they could claim to be *ultra vires* government.

Whilst we can appreciate the robustness of the American Constitution we need not build an idealized conception of such a very human and fallible system. Herbert Agar wrote:

America has failed again and again to create a free society: yet the thing that impresses me about America today is her will to return to that lost fight.[10]

That America has been able to return to the fight is in no small part due to the idea of limited sovereignty which she derived from earlier English rejection of absolute monarchy.

In Britain liberal optimists of the past, in resting both the absolute authority of the State and the safeguarding of individual rights solely on the will of the sovereign people exercised at a general election, seldom paused to think how such omni-competence would, in fact, work.

All effectively organized private bodies governed by their membership separate in their constitutional arrangements power over day-to-day administration, which can be delegated to an elected executive, from the power reserved to the whole membership as being fundamental to the continuing life of the society. Yet at a general election the citizen elector in this country is supposed to be able to separate the 'bread and butter' questions and the deeper constitutional issues which are more often than not deliberately confused.

Part of the value of a written Constitution to a democracy is that it underlines the difference in quality between proposals which are directed towards the solution of immediate problems of Government and those which go to the root of the system by which Parliamentary democracy and private liberty are at once secured.

I referred above to Dicey's opinion as to the written Constitution of the United States as producing 'conservative sentiment' and commanding 'superstitious reverence'. But in the light of history, who would claim that the United States would today be at the centre of the free world if the authority of the Supreme Court and the power of the Senate had been so reduced that all power in the State would rest upon the President countered only by a House of Representatives subject to biennial elections.

The future of the Upper House in Britain is, by analogy, relevant to the consideration of any reform of the Constitution.

The movement for a new constitutional settlement which is beginning to make itself apparent must, in my view, start with a. consideration of reform of the Second Chamber.

We should realize that a Government in control of a Single Chamber could claim, as Cromwell was never able to claim after the execution of King Charles I, legitimacy for all its actions as being done under the undisputed authority and absolute power descended to it through the evolution of our Constitution. Indeed, such a Government could establish precedents for almost any action which it might wish to take—to extend its life *sine die*, to govern under emergency powers, to imprison without trial, to confiscate property without compensation, to tax with extreme discriminatory purposes.

There would be no need for such a Government coming to

power in circumstances which are an ever present contingency to offer as an excuse for its measures a threat to the State from external enemies as in the two world wars of this century. It would only be necessary for it to create a situation of crisis, and so justify its recourse to emergency powers. It could produce such a situation by a retreat from the European Community, followed by the imposition of strict controls over the economy such as were imposed in World War II. It would then be simple to identify as criminal any actions which could be, on the Government's own definition, described as dangerous to the State. The fact that this situation is not a futurist dream but a stark possibility should help us concentrate our minds on a reform of our political system, including a reform of the House of Lords. For this last is likely to become the most active of our constitutional problems.

As at present constituted that House is virtually without authority to act, however unconstitutional the measures proposed by an unfettered House of Commons. It is therefore timely to dwell now for a short space upon its replacement. Indeed, I do not see how a connected scheme of constitutional change could omit a solution of the problem of the powers and composition of a new Second Chamber.

There are two underlying considerations. First, since in our system the Ministry sits in Parliament, and is dependent upon a majority in the Commons, the Second Chamber must not rival the Commons. Secondly, it should represent areas of interest or regions which are not, and never can be, represented in the Commons. I should, therefore, advocate some form of proportional representation as the basis for its election.

I do not thereby imply that a parallel system should be adopted for the Commons. I see it as an advantage that the electorate should have to choose a government by the exercise of a sharp choice between alternatives.

As to the powers of the Second Chamber, these must be adequate to support what I hope will emerge, a new constitutional settlement.

I foresee the power of a new Second Chamber being related in part at least to this important task. But I am sure that a new Second Chamber, however reformed, could not bear the full weight of maintaining a new constitutional settlement. We must look deeper into the whole problem of how to achieve this.

In his Hamlyn Lectures (from which I have quoted above) Lord Scarman makes some very searching comments about our institutions. He puts us on inquiry and leads us to ask whether our long-lasting complex of custom and statute is any longer adequate to modern needs.

If we pursue our studies as to the present state of the law, we shall discover how far we have already been carried by events in at least one unfamiliar direction.

The Universal Declaration of Human Rights was adopted by the United Nations thirty years ago, in 1948. The Declaration itself has no legal authority, but the European Convention for the Protection of Human Rights and Fundamental Freedoms implementing the Universal Declaration is its offspring and was adopted by the Council of Europe in 1950. The United Kingdom was the first nation to ratify that Convention.

But how much thought has been given to the effects on our system of law which must arise from the creation of the Commission of Human Rights[11] and the Court of Human Rights under the European Convention?

Human Rights and Fundamental Freedoms have meant little to us here during this long interval. If we have thought about them at all, it is to hope that these institutions would be barred from entering the United Kingdom by the English Channel. We forget that both the Commission and the Court together represent a powerful idea, the idea of human rights, and that ideas have wings.

Of the inter-action between human rights and the English legal system, Lord Scarman said:

This may be difficult stuff for the Common Law. Charters, Constitutions, broadly generalised Declarations of Right, just do not fit.

And he adds:

It is the helplessness of the law in the face of the legislative Sovereignty of Parliament which makes it difficult for the legal system to accommodate the concept of fundamental and inviolable human rights.

The relevant parts of the three Treaties—of Rome, of Paris and the Euratom Treaty—are already English law and the volume of this part of our law is now considerable. This has gone largely unnoticed because its impact has not yet been great.

But the source of this new law is outside Parliament and outside the United Kingdom and the law relates to private individuals as well as to governments. The style is new to us and so are the principles of interpretation.

Lord Scarman reminds us that Lord Denning, in the Court of Appeal, when examining the impact of the new law and of the new Court (the European Court) on English law, found the new system to be based on statutes differently drafted from English statutes, more general, less detailed and less complex than the English model, and on principles of interpretation giving the courts the role of ensuring the intents of the statutes are not defeated by obscurities, ambiguities or omissions—a role which includes the power to bridge gaps by 'judicial legislation'.

In a word, almost in a fit of absentmindedness, we have already admitted into our midst exotic legal precepts of law conceived on principles which do not allow that a supreme legislature should have the power to make any law which conflicts with the *jus gentium*. There is, therefore, already a hidden conflict which must before long emerge.

A similar conflict underlies any scheme of devolution of power to parts of the United Kingdom, whether to Scotland, Northern Ireland or Wales or to the regions of England.

The failure of the first attempt to devolve power to Scottish and Welsh Assemblies by one Act of Parliament is significant not so much because it found insufficient support in Parliament as because even if the Bill had become law the structure of the proposed scheme was such that it could not possibly endure for long. Its architects had not yet learned how to dig the constitutional foundations upon which any form of divided or circumscribed sovereignty must be founded.

Conflicts between legislature and legislature, and between citizen and governments are necessarily implicit in any scheme of devolution of power to regions. If they are to be peacefully resolved this can only be achieved by judicial means through a

Court of Law protected from the power of Parliament to overturn its decisions. In other words the principle of limited sovereignty in the system will inevitably have to be admitted to our Constitution.

However, we should be false to the cause of freedom under the law if we were to claim that our country's multifarious problems could all be solved by a new constitutional settlement such as I am proposing.

The roots of our difficulties lie in ourselves and in our history. For it is much easier to remove mountains than to alter longstanding habits of mind.

But in so far as our problems are structural, I have offered in this essay a critical examination of the Constitution of the United Kingdom, its historical development, its defects and its potentialities for good or ill.

My purpose throughout has been to relate our Constitution to the overriding purpose of re-creating here a free and plural society.

The present trends, if persisted in, will before long result in the opposite of a free society living under the Rule of Law. If we neglect to reverse these we shall defeat the objects for which our forebears made great sacrifices and to which the majority of our people remain attached.

Moreover, it is no accident that our 'radicals', so called, are to be found on the side of constitutional conservatism. They are continuing to gain great advantages from the defects of our present system. For it conserves for their use the growing power which is flowing from freedom into collectivism.

The philosophy of centralized State-power is now widely recognized by many examples to be the most reactionary which has ever afflicted mankind. It is reactionary because it operates in direct opposition to the freedom of the human spirit.

Its aim is to confine that spirit within the prison of collectivist dogma, and to restrict human action within the limits predetermined by an all-powerful government machine. It is conforming to the pattern of tyranny through the ages.

Thirty years ago the experience of totalitarianism was so fresh in men's minds that the Human Rights Movement received a great impetus. In the moral and political climate of that time the Universal Declaration of Human Rights[12] was conceived and born.

It is necessary to gain an understanding of the basis of the Declaration, that is, the unique value of the human person and a determination to establish this in the post-war world.

This can best be grasped by reading the second paragraph of the preamble to the Declaration, together with Articles 6 and 7.

The second paragraph runs thus:

Whereas disregard and contempt for human rights have resulted in barbarous acts, which have outraged the conscience of mankind, and the advent of a world in which human beings shall enjoy freedom of speech and belief and freedom from fear and want has been proclaimed as the highest aspiration of the common people. . . .

Article 6 thus:

Everyone has the right to recognition everywhere as a person before the law.

And Article 7 thus:

All are equal before the law and are entitled without discrimination to equal protection of the law. All are entitled to equal protection against any discrimination in violation of this Declaration and against any incitement to such discrimination.

Thus the Declaration was founded upon the presumption of the value of the human being as an individual, and not on the concept of men and women as mere units within the collectivist State. Memories of secret police, concentration camps and forced labour were still green in the Western world of 1948.

After a further generation of experience, it is not hard to perceive why the freedoms which the Declaration wished to assure to all mankind are still not enjoyed by the majority of the peoples of the world.

There was inherent in the Declaration a conflict between opposing and irreconcilable ideas about the nature of man and his destiny.

The character of that conflict, then largely disguised, is now manifest. It is a conflict which should be plain to all within these Islands who have eyes to see and minds to understand. It is a conflict within our unwritten Constitution itself.

Professor Lauterpacht in *International Law and Human Rights* has summed up the case for the special protection of human rights in these words:

Democracy, although an essential condition of freedom, is not an absolute safeguard to it. That safeguard must be outside and above the State.

I have dealt at some length upon the present condition of our Constitution and on the dangers to liberty inherent in both the theory and practice of the absolute authority which it gives to an all-powerful legislature.[13]

I look upon that task as being more important, at least for the layman, than an attempt at 'Constitution-mongering'.

A new constitutional settlement on the lines I envisage can only be devised as the result of deep thought, great experience and the operation of time.

By a long historical process Britain has evolved a system of common law which has proved serviceable to many widely differing peoples in many parts of the world, with their own habits of thought, religious beliefs, social traditions and customary behaviour.

Rarely, if ever, has our country deliberately imposed upon a dependency an all-embracing revision of its existing legal system. She has acted upon the fundamental assumption that not only at home but elsewhere 'law has no gaps or omissions, only a few silences'. Our lawyers have thus found means to break these silences in ways acceptable to local preconceptions and so to offer to each dependency its own Rule of Law.

All this now belongs to history.

In yielding independence we have, as we have already seen, gone beyond customary law in constitutional matters and have supplied, or at least advised upon, models for written Constitutions.

We have learned from history what ought to be done by other nations whilst omitting to apply these lessons of experience to ourselves.

But from that experience we can identify a number of essential features necessary for the workings of a written Constitution for Britain. These at the least are:

1   A Bill of Rights (replacing the Bill of Rights of 1689)
2   A bicameral legislature with a defined relationship between the two Houses of Parliament
3   Entrenched provisions, including the Bill of Rights, with restraints upon unlimited administrative and legislative power
4   A system of reference to the electorate by mandatory referendum, the method to be determined in the Constitution and not available for modification by the Government of the day
5   A Constitutional Court in which would reside the ultimate right of adjudication on constitutional matters
6   Codification of the law by a gradual process which would complete the system of statute law which can no longer be regarded as a mere elucidation of the Common Law
7   The setting up of machinery to watch over and to develop our system of law, with special reference to administrative law, thereby restoring the unity and universality of the legal system

Learned opinion appears to differ over whether or not Parliament can, by the normal processes of legislation, institute a written Constitution which could effectively limit its own unfettered sovereignty.

This problem is capable of solution. Most important is the creation of a will to reform. This was manifest in the early nineteenth century and resulted in the first Reform Act of 1832.

To modify existing forms rather than create entirely new institutions has enabled us to maintain continuity in constitutional development.

Thus the Constitutional Court could be formed out of the existing Judicial Committee of the Privy Council, a body with great authority and long experience.

Moreover, subject to appeal, constitutional questions with limited reference could be adjudicated by the lower Courts.

Against the background of a Bill of Rights and entrenched

provisions, our legal system, which has shown itself capable of adaptation, could by processes intelligible alike to Parliament, the administrator and the citizen, be remoulded in conformity with constitutional restraints upon unlimited power.

Thus would the balance be restored within the national community, between the authority of the State and private rights—a balance which the Human Rights Movement insistently demands and which will not be denied.

1   S. A. de Smith: *Constitutional and Administrative Law 1971* (London, 1971): '. . . During its declining years the Colonial Office moved from apathy or hostility towards this idea (full-scale entrenched bills of rights, based on the general pattern of the European Convention) and began actively to press it on colonial politicians. The unmentionable became indispensable. What was obnoxious to the Westminster model is now the glory of Westminster's export models.'

2   Sir Leslie Scarman: Hamlyn Lectures, twenty-sixth series: *English Law—the New Dimension* (and Scarman passim)

3   A. V. Dicey, KC: *Law of the Constitution*, eighth edition, 1914

4   House of Lords: Gouriet and Others (Respondents) *v.* HM Attorney-General (Appellant) et al. Verbatim report, 26 July 1977

5   The Rt. Hon. Lord Shawcross, QC: Letter to *The Times*, 3 August 1977

6   Lord Fraser of Tullybelton. See also Lord Dilhorne's comments in the same case on the role of the Attorney-General

7   Court of Appeal: Gouriet *v.* Union of Post Office Workers, Post Office Engineering Union and HM Attorney-General. Verbatim report, 27 January 1977

8   The *New Law Journal*, Thursday 4 August 1977

9   Mr T. Jackson wrote an article in *The Times* (8 June 1977) under the heading 'How the Judges Declared Open Season on the Unions for Right Wing Hunters'. He concluded thus: 'If the Court of Appeal's decision is upheld (in the Lords) then consideration would have to be given to further Parliamentary legislation to ensure that the benefits and immunities conferred by the recent acts are fully upheld.' Evidently Mr Jackson has been led to believe that the Attorney-General's prerogative to give or not to give his *fiat* in a case brought to prevent Unions from committing criminal offences is one of 'the benefits and immunities' enjoyed by trade unions. In the event his fear of losing this 'benefit' was proved groundless.

10 Quoted in Ferguson and McHenry: *The American Federal Constitution* (New York)

11 On 29 July 1977 the European Commission on Human Rights ruled that despite a decision in the House of Lords which upheld an appeal by the Attorney-General from a decision in the Court of Appeal, the British Government in attempting to prevent the publication of an article in the *Sunday Times* had violated Article 10 of the European Convention. The case will now go before the European Court of Human Rights

12 See Professor H. Lauterpacht, QC: *International Law and Human Rights* (London, 1950)

13 Lord Hailsham, with his customary force, has said: 'I have now come to the conclusion that our Constitution is wearing out. Its central defects are gradually coming to outweigh its merits, and its central defects consist in the absolute power we confer on our sovereign body . . . I envisage nothing less than a written Constitution for the United Kingdom.' Rt. Hon. Lord Hailsham of Marylebone, CH: Dimbleby Lecture, 14 October 1976

John Gouriet

Freedom and Enterprise

THE MARKET, THE CONSUMER, THE PEOPLE

The development of inflationary difficulties, rising unemployment and instability in international monetary and trade relations in the mid 1970s have, almost inevitably, resulted in a comparable flood of books and articles proclaiming the end of the capitalist system. This is natural and to be expected since for over a century now the fundamental economic debate has been between those who support a free enterprise, market economy, with all its imperfections, and those who champion a planned economy on the grounds that it will both abolish instabilities and improve the general lot of mankind through controlled distribution, because of its alleged greater efficiency. Ideologically the main conflict has been between those who can best be described as 'liberal democrats' or conservatives with a small 'c' versus those who are the heirs of Marx and Engels.

Logically there would seem to be four areas of social development which need to be examined. These are:

1   The nature of pre-Industrial Society
2   The experience of the Industrial Revolution
3   The achievements and weaknesses of the so-called capitalist system

4   The achievements and weaknesses of the centrally planned economy, with special reference to the Soviet experience.

Only when this ground has been covered can worthwhile conclusions be drawn.

The condition of mankind without capitalism, without industry, without the technology it has created, has been portrayed by romantic historians as a lost golden age. There has never been a 'golden age', and not too many generations ago, people were familiar with 'continual fear and danger of violent death; and the life of man, solitary, poor, nasty, brutish and short'.[1] Before we consider the real and undisputed suffering and hard times endured during the Industrial Revolution, it would be worth looking into the history of earlier centuries. For example, Samuel Pepys described a visit to the Perkins family of Parson's Drove in Huntingdonshire in his diary on 17 September 1663: 'a heathen place where I found my uncle and aunt Perkins and their daughters, poor wretches, in a sad poor thatched cottage like a poor barn or stable peeling of damp'.

Or, if there is some gilt remaining to this age, consider the great famine of 1314–18 which afflicted most of continental Europe, when in the Amsterdam of 1315–16 the price of grain rose by 300%! Later at the very worst point of the Industrial Age, at the height of the Napoleonic wars (when the market was distorted by the inflationary restriction of continental exports to this country) the price of wheat was to touch 128 shillings per quarter, it was thus roughly, and very briefly, 100% up on what it had been in pre-war conditions.

History is in fact studded with starvation riots. They are something different in kind both from the political disturbances of modern times and even from such mid-nineteenth-century outbreaks as the Hyde Park riots of the early 1860s which so agitated Matthew Arnold. A political demonstration, however justified and however angry, at any time since the Napoleonic Wars (and in the view of some economic historians, since an earlier date) is something different in kind from the starvation riots which are the punctuation marks of pre-industrial, pre-capitalist history. The operative word is *starvation*, and the commodity at issue is bread or some other staple food. The bread riots of Milan in 1628 which Manzoni retold in *I Promessi Sposi*, the riots at Newbury in 1766 when the price of bread was temporarily brought down by violence, or those which occurred in Cornwall across the eighteenth century when granaries and cornmills were recurringly destroyed by the mob, are all instances of what pre-industrial man was heir to.

But perhaps the most graphic illustration of that general poverty which existed before the Capitalist Industrial Revolution is to be seen in Ireland. That country which the successive statutes, monopolies and prohibitions of a Parliament, subordinate to English interests, together with other random factors, had excluded from almost all industrial development, continued as an agricultural economy (and a monoculture at that) into recent times.

The poverty of nineteenth-century Ireland is often tied in with the general harshness of industrial life in that century. When that happens it is very important to remember that in talking about the Irish famine, we are invariably to be found discussing the events of the mid 1840s and specifically 1847. In that unforgettable year $3\frac{1}{2}\%$ of the population of Ireland died as a result of starvation. However in the forgotten famine of 1739 which did not surprise or disturb pre-industrial man, an estimate of not less than 20% of the Irish people died of hunger![2] In consequence, when the Irish population expanded again, it provided men so accustomed to a medieval standard of poverty that when an English labourer, rightly in our eyes, looked upon six shillings a week as a starvation wage, Irishmen were prepared to work for half a crown. However hard-working and poor the English labourer was, the rural Irish could out-work him and under-live him. Of all the sorrows of Ireland, perhaps the one least observed and most greatly to be lamented was that she was not exploited by industrialists.

According to Professor Braudel,[3] 'a privileged country like France is said to have experienced thirteen famines in the 16th century, eleven in the 17th, and sixteen in the 18th.' And what human experience do the silent statistics convey? To take a relatively mild example, beggars from distant provinces, verminous and covered with fleas descended upon the town of Troyes in 1573.[4] The resolution of the town councillors was that they must be put outside the town.

... to do this, an ample amount of bread was baked to be distributed among the aforesaid poor who would be assembled at one of the gates of the town without being told why, and after the distribution to each one of his bread and a piece of silver, they would be made to leave the town by the aforesaid gate which would be closed on the last one, and it would be indicated to them over the town walls that they should not return to the aforesaid Troyes before the new grain from the next harvest. This was done. After the gifts the dismayed poor were driven from the town of Troyes ...

Or to take a harsher instance,[5] one observer in what is now Eastern France, recorded in 1652: 'the people of Lorraine and other surrounding lands are reduced to such extremities that, like animals, they eat the grass in the meadows ... and (they) are as black and thin as skeletons.'

If this were not bad enough, the conditions in such countries as India were worse. A Dutch merchant left us an account of the general famine in that continent in 1630–31:[6]

People wandered hither and thither helpless, having abandoned their towns and villages. Their condition could be recognised immediately: sunken eyes, wan faces, lips flecked with foam, lower jaw projecting, bones protruding through the skin; and these poor people would reach the point of despair at which they cut open the stomachs of the dead to eat their entrails. Hundreds of thousands died [and] the country was covered with corpses which stayed unburied and such a stink arose that the air was filled with it and pestilential.

In contrast, the question should perhaps be considered how far the history of outrage at the suffering endured in the course of the Industrial Revolution is in fact the history of a growing susceptibility and humanity which an advancing industrial society, a far cry from the immediate prospect of death in a ditch, had made possible for its heirs.

The Industrial Revolution and the Agrarian Revolution, which is entangled with it, together removed the countries they affected from that promiscuous mortality which had been the unremarked condition of the 'golden age' which preceded them. However, to bring home the realities of harder times before the *Hard Times* of which Dickens and other commentators of the nineteenth century wrote is not to flinch from nor to soften the severity of that age.

The '300,000 little girls in Lancashire from whose labour if we only deduct two hours a day, away goes the wealth, away goes the capital, away go the resources, the power and the glory of England'—to quote William Cobbett's speech in Parliament on the eve of the Factory Act of 1833—should not be left for oblivion. Neither should the conditions of gross overcrowding which marred the nineteenth century (something not to be excused because it had already existed in the non-industrial early eighteenth century, in London at least). The Industrial Revolution which was surely made even harsher than it might have been by the twenty years of war with France from 1792 to 1815 was marked by industrial and rural unrest with which civilized man would find it difficult not to sympathize.

Even here bad was made worse by the survival into the industrial age of certain interventionist policies from the mercantile past. The Hammonds, who in 'The Bleak Age' gave the grimmest account of industrial England, point to an income of £22 for a labourer of which no less than £11. 7s. 7d. was taken up (and thus taken out of his purchasing power) by indirect taxes.[7] Such taxation is a pre-industrial survival, not the doing of capitalism. The poverty and harshness of the urban and industrial world—the long hours, the factory discipline, the overcrowded houses, the industrial diseases are recorded history; and the best testifiers against them are the men who worked to reform and ameliorate them (Shaftesbury, Ostler, Sadler and Salt, all of them part of the system!) As evils they must not be reduced to cold statistical exegesis as one school of optimist economic historians desires, seeking to imply that the Industrial Revolution did not hurt; neither however, should such suffering be used as the 'pessimist' school seems to wish—as a sort of cash crop to be farmed in the Marxist cause. To those who lived through the period, the central years of the Industrial Revolution were like a tunnel. To determine the length of the tunnel one can argue the toss about comparative wage rates and price rates, even follow Dr Hartwell to discover the weight and number of animals slaughtered for food at Smithfield, and still be uncertain whether the standard of living rose or fell fractionally or just dithered. One would also do well to remember pauper apprenticeships and those three hundred thousand little girls in Lancashire. But somewhere in the early 1840s there appeared a steady and indisputable change in the condition of the working people of England. Their standard of living and real wages had, beyond any dispute, begun a relentless course of improvement.

It was the English-based German Socialist Eduard Bernstein, the chronicler of industrial poverty, the friend and disciple of Friedrich Engels, who rejected the 'sclerosis of dogma' and pointed out the rising standard of living assured by mass-produced goods and the cheap food of high agricultural technology. Or to take Waltershausen's figures for Germany, a later industrializer: annual sugar consumption per person in 1870: 12 pounds, in 1907: 34 pounds; beer: 78 litres in 1872, 123 in 1900; meat: 59 pounds in 1873, 105 pounds in 1912.[8]

Capitalism is as capitalism does, and the ultimate truth about it as a system is that, to paraphrase Eduard Bernstein's argument, the rich grow richer *and the poor also grow richer*. In the process, unfortunately some sections of the poor got poorer first which lent fuel to the lie. But nowhere so notably as where they clung to a craft which was capable of being outperformed by new machinery. A classic example is of handloom weavers whose standard of living did indeed fall drastically. John Kay had invented the flying shuttle in 1733. It was bitterly resented since it was capable of doing the work of half a dozen men. (In a rather similar spirit the introduction of High Oxygen furnaces, which are universal in West Germany, has been resisted and hampered for years in this country making the British Steel Corporation the wretchedly uncompetitive body it is.) Kay narrowly avoided being lynched on one occasion, but eventually, in the late 1760s, the flying shuttle, the very first of the technological innovations of the textile industry began to be used by the mill owners of the North West. Before the industrial era, weaving and spinning of woollens and fustian (cotton and linen mixed) had been carried on in dozens of districts. There was no narrow concentration in Lancashire, the West Riding and the West of Scotland, but cloth was produced as far apart as Kent and Westmorland. Perhaps the most thriving districts were East Anglia and the South West, with Lancashire emerging as a strong competitor. Daniel Defoe in his *Tour Through the Whole Island of Great Britain*[9] which was written in 1723, forty years before the Industrial Revolution, praises Manchester as 'the greatest mere village in England . . . as at Frome in Somersetshire the town is extended in a surprising manner'. But Frome itself, Defoe writes, 'is so prodigiously increased within these last twenty or thirty years that . . . it is very likely to be one of the greatest and wealthiest inland towns in England.' All this through a flourishing textile trade.

Now the resistance to technology varied in different parts of England, and the handloom weavers of Frome described by Defoe back in the 'golden age' as 'poor people', objected most bitterly. Indeed long after the last of the four great inventions of the cloth trade—the power loom—had been created by Edmund Cartwright in 1794, the handloom weavers of Frome were still resisting the flying shuttle, first designed in 1733. Their last riot against it was in 1819.

Consequently the 'great and wealthy inland town' has today a population of just over 13,000 while the wages of handloom weavers had fallen by 1830 to about one-fifth of what they had been in 1800. A more powerful *memento mori* for a country like ours with a contemporary Luddite compulsion to resist new technology and to spin out low productivity payrolls could hardly be imagined. The weaver of Frome could repair his fortunes by going to Lancashire. The inference for the British Steel Corporation's employees and others is there to be drawn.

Without going on interminably about pig iron production, as Stalin used to do, the essential answer to human suffering as human numbers have grown has been technology. Swift once observed that the man who made two blades of grass grow where one grew before would be worth the whole race of politicians. There have in fact been generations of such men beginning in Swift's own lifetime. Most history classes have included fleeting mention of 'Turnip' Townshend, but the full importance of

Charles Townshend as a double-grass grower is rarely remembered.

At the start of the eighteenth century it was estimated that a quarter of England and Wales—ten million acres—was wasteland, fen, moorland and, in the eastern part of the country, had soil too sandy to cultivate. Townshend learned from the experience of Holland, whose limited space and marsh soil had obliged farmers to innovate or go under. His own estate was made up of barren, sandy, and swamp-laden land in backwoods Norfolk, 'where two rabbits struggled for every blade of grass'. He produced with clay and lime dressings (marl) a good-quality soil. By four-course rotation—of wheat, turnips, barley and clover, he abolished the old fallow season and (since clover transfers nitrogen to the soil) was able to produce food for humans or animals every year instead of two years in three, while making it possible to feed a higher proportion of livestock during the winter.

It had been the custom to:

> Sow four grains in a row
> One for the pigeon, one for the crow
> One to rot and one to grow.

However, Townshend's contemporary, Jethro Tull, introduced the seed drill which placed seeds deep enough in the ground and spaced far enough apart for them to flourish. Together they answered Swift's epigram, by ensuring that grain grew, and in quantity, where it had never grown before.

The English agricultural revolution is only one wave of technological change in a succession down to the recent 'green revolution'. The refrigerator ship and the railway freight truck defeated the English farmer in the open market by transporting a cheaper product from the Canadian prairies and the South American pampas in the 1880s. They were part of a second relay of innovation and the beneficiary was the British industrial worker. Since it is an uncontested platitude of economic life that the poorer an individual or family is, the higher the proportion of income which is spent on foodstuffs (and specifically on staples such as bread), those who benefited most by agricultural technology, and the falling food prices which accompanied it, were the poorer people.

If grain was costing something in the region of 126 shillings a quarter at one point during the Napoleonic Wars, it had dropped as low as 17/4 by 1894—half the price it had been in the mid-eighteenth century and just over one third of the price at the outbreak of the Napoleonic Wars. In consequence of this and other developments, standards of living steadily and relentlessly rose for most people.

According to Professor Rostow[10] the standard of living rose on average in the last quarter of the nineteenth century by about 2% a year—we are talking here about real wages, actual spending power. Even if the fairly heavy unemployment of the period is fed into the calculation to depreciate the figure, the performance of capitalism is still a year-on-year increase of 1·85%. It was the rising standard of living (in fact it had been rising since mid-century), which so depressed the followers of Marx as unequivocal evidence against the Master's theory that by some implacable mechanism the poor must get poorer until the point of explosion and political revolution.

The point which should also be made is that this country was only able to afford to become a major importer of grain and meat by reason of her successful manufacturing industry. And they in turn were the creatures of technology. Without it, as in the long ages of changeless sterile poverty, we should have enjoyed, if that is quite the word, the grim insufficiency of the medieval peasant with his primitive dwelling, susceptibility to disease, short life and low threshold of minimal expectations. The industrial technology which paid for imported food and which allowed the standard of living of an Englishman to increase by half in twenty-five years was the same technology which created the 'dark satanic mills'.

The pattern of industrial development is not identical throughout the world. Britain had the experience of acting as a pilot ship of capitalism for all the other countries. In the process she took the lead but she also made mistakes from which countries starting later, like Germany and Sweden, were to learn. What does not cease to impress is the sheer exhilarating

momentum with which slow and laborious procedures became
no longer goods for the market, but goods for the nation and
soon goods for the world. The Shuttle, the Jenny, the Water
Frame (the last two later combined in Crompton's Mule), and
the Power Loom, the first invented in 1733, the last in 1794,
were, with steam power, the principal weapons of the Industrial
Revolution. The cost of producing cotton yarn fell between 1779
and 1812 by a mere 90%. By these savings and by those which
were created by Darby's coal smelting process, by the Newcomen
and then the Watt steam engine, and by Henry Cort's pud-
dling and rolling process, a great multiple of the previous output
of goods was produced.

But such advances were possible on the basis of individual
decisions. The forgone consumption on savings was the basis
for investment. And by investment we mean the purchase of
plant and machinery in order to extend and multiply the production of goods—the very growth by which a higher standard
of living, a wider range of commodities becomes available to the
ordinary citizen.

The knack of accumulation and ploughing back for larger
scale production is neatly portrayed in the records of Samuel
Walker of Rotherham:[11]

1741   In or about October ... Saml. and Aaron Walker built
an Air Furnace on the old nailer's smithy on the back
side of Saml. Walker's cottage at Grenoside ... and the furnace once more began to proceed a little, Saml. Walker
teaching the School at Grenoside and Aaron Walker making
nails and shearing etc. part of his time.

1743   Aaron Walker now began to be pretty much employed and
had 4 shillings a week to live upon ...

1745   This year Saml. Walker finding business increase, was
obliged to give up his school ... then we allowed ourselves
ten shillings a week each for wages to maintain our families.

Add to a value by now of £400 for the business a further
£200 from savings, including £50 from John Crawshaw, who
had previously been employed 'at 12 pence a day', and a steel
casting house could be set up at Masborough, then a ware-
house, then a river barge, then a navigable cut to the river.

The Walkers allowed themselves their first dividend in 1757—£140, and capital was relentlessly ploughed back. By 1812 the assets of Samuel Walker and Co., and an associate company, Walker and Booth, were jointly valued at £354,000.

That was capitalism that was!

The first rule of understanding the society which we take for granted and whose standards of generally diffused wealth are beneath our undiscerning noses, is to measure the material achievement. To cite Dr Fabricant's figures:[12] in the United States between 1899 and 1937 the output of petroleum, milk and beet sugar rose by more than 1000%, the increase in output of cement, canned fruit and vegetables was only very slightly below 1000%. As for motor cars, there were 8,000 private cars in the United States in 1900; in 1940 there were more than 27 million! Per million of the population there were only 100 cars in 1900; in 1940 there were 207,000. There had been one car for every ten thousand, by the end of the thirties there was one for every five. Yet this was the state of affairs after a decade of severe depression, a depression which had provided left-wing publicists with their own cottage industry of homespun outrage.

A profoundly dishonest emotional trick has been played by left-wing social historians and by such phenomena as Chaplin's film *Modern Times* in their portrayal of the America of Henry Ford as a kind of jazzed-up aceldama in which the victim (the worker) was the slave of a monstrous conveyor belt so that he lived the life of a sort of high-speed galley slave to no apparent purpose.

In fact it is worth comparing the tone of left-wing propaganda in the past—'crushing the workers under the iron heel of capitalism' and so on, with that of the New Left (which dates from the late 1950s)—the crises of 'admass', affluence and the 'sick society' all of which terms concede the basic premise that they are actually talking about a country with a very high standard of living for the great mass of its people. A standard achieved in spite, rather than because, of Left-wing activities.

The terms of most bitter abuse in the left-wing lexicon are confessions of their failure. Take 'suburban' for example. To anyone except a Neanderthal reactionary believing that 'workers should

be kept in their place', the idea of industrial workers living in five-
or six-room semi-detached houses rather than an industrial bar-
racks may seem wholly estimable. However the Marxist, like the
ultra-reactionary, has a certain nostalgia for squalor.

There is a certain disposition, especially among left wingers
who are themselves long used to the quality of life customary in
Long Island or Hampstead, to be patronizing about washing
machines, colour television, deep freezes and food mixers while
becoming quietly paranoid about the motor car. These are the
goods not only of technology but of capitalism. They are the products which the market, or the consumer, or the people elect to
have. Manifestly they represent an enormous improvement in
the standard of living from the days of the mangle, the sampler,
the wire meat-safe, an hour's work with a wooden spoon in a
basin and the pleasure of going always and everywhere on foot.
In every sense that has meaning they represent a liberation for
the citizen and especially his wife. They stick in the throat of progressive opinion, not because they are not beneficial (you would
need to be a little bit out of your mind actually to be *against*
washing machines), but because they are part of the process by
which the general primary poverty under which men lived for
most of recorded history has been defeated by the profit motive.
The revolution therefore must be induced, for there is insufficient poverty to ignite it unaided.

When we talk about our problems and our economic difficulties, which are not disputed, we must first of all recognize that
they exist on a totally different plane from those of seventy years
ago, and in a dimension utterly different from that experienced
by, for example, citizens of the USSR. Any form of social
organization is to be judged by the goods it produces. The Western democracies are maintaining a flow of consumer goods as unknown to history as to the Soviet Union. And even in the
circumstances of recession and unemployment the purchasing
power in the hands of those out of work is as a general rule higher
than that of Soviet workers fully employed.

The average Soviet wage stood officially in 1972 at 130
roubles per month (the minimum being 60 roubles). According
to Professor Wiles[13] the conversion rate from the grotesque

official Soviet Rate of 2·16 roubles to the pound varies between the (illegal) Soviet Free Market of anything between 12 and 15 to the pound and the London Free Market (illegal in Soviet Law) of 8–10 roubles to the pound.

All discussion of Soviet purchasing power is difficult not least because the regime by a system of privileges, foreign exchange shops, holidays for Party Members and other élite persons and the system of *blat* or contacts for obtaining otherwise unobtainable goods make it so. There is good reason to think that Disraeli's trinity of untruths should be replaced by four new degrees—lies, damned lies, statistics and Soviet statistics. Even so on this estimate the Soviet worker in receipt of average earnings is rubbing shoulders with the lower end of the unemployed scale in Britain.

Czechoslovakia, a country which had a sound industrial base before the Soviet takeover in 1948, and is closer to the West in experience and comparative standards than any other country of Eastern Europe is an instructive case. During the Prague Spring of 1968, people were not only demanding liberty of conscience and opinion, they were complaining of the low standard of living and of an unequivocal failure to deliver the goods.

Otto Schmidt[14] in *Literarni Listy* of 23 May 1968 made a comparative calculation (in Czech crowns) of the average industrial wage:

USA	10,400
Sweden	5,900
UK	4,170
W. Germany	3,560
Austria	2,250
France	2,250
Czechoslovakia	1,448

This in a country inheriting an industrial base and after twenty years of Marxist Socialism. When it came to those holding technical and scientific qualifications, the results (again in Czech crowns) were even more depressing:

USA	21,000
France	12,900

Czechoslovakia   2,000

A particular source of bitterness was the disparity between production and consumption. The language used by classical Marxism to describe capitalism—the exploitation of the workers, the holding of wages at an iron minimum—was exactly true of conditions in Czechoslovakia.

The achievement of the Communist system, whether in the USSR or in the countries which share the pains and the penalties of Comecon, the East European Common Market, is not inconsiderable, but what the ordinary citizen receives bears no comparison with the preferential treatment given to the Military High Command. The way things are achieved is also totally different. At the basis of Soviet economics is what Michael Polanyi memorably called 'Command Planning'—the authority of the parade ground continued in civilian life, but reinforced with sanctions rather more formidable than the glasshouse.

The command economy is very good at concentrating on a narrow front to achieve a handful of specific objectives. The building of Admiral Gorschkov's terrifying nuclear submarine fleet with a new vessel being produced rather more often than once a month is a case in point.

Leaving aside the despicable death camps of the Gulag, it is worth listing some of the other sanctions available to those in command.[15] In 1930 a decree forbidding the free movement of labour was passed, followed two months later by another forbidding factories to employ those who had left their previous employment without permission. Unemployment relief was abolished on the (untrue) grounds 'that there was no more unemployment'. It is rather like the British Government refusing to pay unemployment benefit to the self-employed on the grounds that they cannot be unemployed. In 1931 the first prison sentences for breaches of labour discipline were introduced into the Soviet Railways; soon came the compulsory labour books for industrial and transport workers (our own 714 Tax Exemption Certificate, with its photograph and licence to trade is not too dissimilar); in March there followed punitive measures for negligence, followed by a species of truck system (the payment in kind most bitterly denounced by radical historians of our Industrial Revolution). In August 1932 the death penalty was brought in for the theft of State or collective property; in November of that year a single day's unauthorized absence became punishable with instant dismissal.

As a final code to what must be the bleakest code of Labour Law in history, one which made the Combination Acts look like a Workers' Charter, there was re-introduced the internal passport, one of the great symbolic evils of Tsarist times. In such an ambience it is not altogether surprising that the head of the Soviet Trade Union Organisation, N. M. Shvernik, did not find such legislation on Industrial Relations to be 'unacceptable'. Indeed he proclaimed as the trade unions' 'most important task' the establishment of piece work on the basis of 'norms', a procedure known to Marx as the exploitation of labour.

Not all labour was so progressive! Dmitri Vitkovski, who worked on and, more remarkably, survived, the building of the White Sea Canal—another crash programme undertaken by the command economy but this time using the forced labour with whose many million servitors Alexander Solzhenitsyn has recently made us familiar—has this to say:[16]

At the end of the work day there were corpses left on the work site. One of them was hunched over beneath an overturned wheelbarrow; he had hidden his hands in his knees and frozen to death in that position. Someone had frozen with his hands between his knees. Two were frozen back to back leaning against each other . . . in their village simplicity they gave all their strength to their work and froze to death embracing in pairs. At night the sledges went out and collected them. The drivers threw the corpses into the sledges . . . in the summer bones remained from corpses which had not been removed in time and . . . they got into the concrete on the last lock at the city of Belomorsk and will be preserved there forever.

This compares with the automatic stoppage of work and the church funeral which followed the death of a navvy working on the railway system in the most implacably laissez-faire sort of capitalism between 1825 and 1845 in Britain. The conditions of death carry fairly clear implications about its frequency.[17] However because of norms and a time limit which had to be met, the

Soviet engineers had to cheat with figures to create the impression of having dug the canal to specification. Today, being only sixteen feet deep, it has no traffic to speak of!

In so far as heavy industry is concerned, pig iron production and other metallurgy, the goods were produced by this ferocious coercion, but they were the goods which the State and its supreme guide and counsellor demanded, *not* the market, *not* the consumer, *not* the people.

Even in industry and with such penal laws against the working class, a great deal could and did go grotesquely wrong, like copper production which was supposed to reach 150,000 tons in a single year and barely touched 50,000 tons. However, what was remarkable about the Socialism practised in the Soviet Union, apart from coercion by factory police, was the cult of the norm or quota. The rewards of capitalism were introduced sideways in the form of bonuses for directors who achieved over 120% of their quotas; and the shock troops of labour—the Stakhanovites—were rewarded *directly by managers* with better rations. Indeed, for a period food supplies were put into the control of factory managers. The despised ameliorators of the English liberalism had made payments in food or other goods illegal in the Truck Acts of 1831.

But if Soviet industry with such a shrivelled carrot and steel-spiked stick was able to make progress (on the narrow front of heavy, militarily related industry which had been assigned to it) the picture in Agriculture was different again; but equally horrifying.

The great Soviet hunger of the 1930s has been described as the only famine ever directly made by man. The application of collectivization was the agrarian parallel to crash industrialization. By command, by centralized decision a plan to collectivize 20% of peasant land became on one day, 5 January 1930, a *complete* collectivization. Within three months in 1930 the number of peasant holdings which were collectivized increased from four million to fourteen million; half the peasant holdings were collectivized within five months. The peasants fought back and slaughtered livestock rather than let it go to the State. At the same time grain was actually *exported*—5 million tons in

1930–31 and 1·75 million tons in the famine year 1932–3. As Ivan Stadnyuk[18] was to write in Russia during the brief Khrushchev thaw—'The men died first, then the children, then the women.' Between five and six million people died, more than half of them in the Ukraine. In the process, Soviet agriculture lost about 25% of its productive capacity. As for modern technology, the amount of power available on the land was actually less in 1938 than it had been in 1929.

At the centre of a human catastrophe equal in its bill of mortality to Hitler's massacre of the Jews, lay the flaw which is to be found at the base of other less macabre Socialist undertakings—the pursuit of political objectives before those of economics. Collectivization was introduced far less for its supposed, and spurious merits, than out of the need to destroy the foundation of the 'class enemy': the kulaks or richer peasants, precisely the rural entrepreneurial class who were most likely, if left to themselves, to invest in electrification, tractors or irrigation—those who in another century or another country would have been taking up four-course rotation and the marling of sandy soils.

The dreadful supremacy of politics over economics is summed up in the words of a high-ranking official, that the harvest of 1933 'was a test of our strength and their endurance. It took a famine to show them who is master here. It has cost millions of lives but the collective farm system is here to stay. We have won the war!'[19]

Such was the victory that in 1953 the number of cattle was actually lower (on the admission of the Soviet authorities themselves) than it had been in 1928 before forced collectivization, and the number of cows alone was less than the figure for 1916![20] Soviet production figures regularly use 1916, the third year of a World War and much worse than 1913, as their basis for modern comparisons. So this particular figure carries implications for Soviet agriculture which are simply terrible. Grain production was slightly higher—15% in the late thirties, not because of technology or socialism but because the area sown was increased by about 10%.

Meanwhile unsocialized agriculture, which amounted in 1937

to 3·3% of the total cultivated area, was providing 21·5% of the total agricultural production of the country. This was despite supposed economies of size and the virtual monopoly of tractors by the collective farms, which had access to the Motor Traction Stations. In fact the oppressed and politically hated private peasant (like the British self-employed today) has been too important to be eliminated altogether, and the most stable of Communist Agricultural systems, that of Kadar's Hungary, is the one which has effectively acknowledged failure and asked peasants quietly to get on with private production.

On top of a great crime there have been great follies, like Mr Kruschev's virgin lands scheme—a desperate gamble, which hardly survived its second year, to grow grain on soil too salty and in circumstances too scrambled and ill managed to yield more than one crop and a limited harvest of short term Public Relations.

The hard truth about sixty years of Socialist agriculture is that where once there were three great grain exporting zones in the world—the Ukraine, the open lands of South America, and the Canadian and US prairies (with the growth of population the South Americans do no better than feed themselves)—the North Americans have increased productivity fourteen-fold since pre-war days, and the Soviets have become, to the utter humiliation of the system they erected, *regular net importers of grain* on a massive scale.

Finally the Russian command system, having chosen to invest in heavy industry, has opted without reference to the market, the consumer or the people, to produce consumer goods which are few, shoddy and expensive; and to make them available so capriciously that woollen sweaters, nylon stockings, even good quality soap, have that status of being a neo-currency which our elders remember from the siege years of the World War II. The USSR has been able under the command structure to achieve very strong growth in heavy industry, but she has also under the terms of that structure, committed by *ukase* a quite disproportionate number of her first-class breakthrough scientists to military affairs and a proportion of GNP for military purposes roughly double that which the US spends.

On an inferior economic base she has been able to create superior military status: but at what cost. If ever there was a supreme military-industrial complex, capitalism did not create it.

The market with all its faults, and subject to both the correction *and* the meddling of an elected Parliament (for example, both Factory Acts and metrication) reacts to demand. If pinball machines and rock records are produced it is because people want them, just as they want and get clothes, food and household liberation machines like tumble dryers and dish washers. It is when market forces are not allowed to operate effectively, by reason of centralized interference and control that problems arise.

The entrepreneur is bidden. If he wants to make money he elects to be the most efficient and effective servant of the consumer, a sort of merchant Figaro. Above all, he is out of politics, or at most on its periphery. He has not the time or the inclination for both and there are too many of him (since Marx was wrong about monopoly as well). Any political power which industry has is diffused. In the West, the entrepreneur has produced wealth in the form of resources, capital and consumer goods according to how well he has understood the commands of the market. His capacity for tyranny is negligible not because of any virtue or benevolence on his part, but because (except in trivialities) the old adage is wrong: money is not power in the political sense, it is the alternative to power.

The capitalist system operating within a great representative democracy is the best known way of making money for the benefit of the majority and providing a safety net for the waifs of society. As a system for exercising political power it usually fails wherever it bothers to try. For example, politicians of all parties have played into the hands of those who wish to replace democracy with drab uniformity by allowing, even encouraging an insupportable volume of public expenditure, although their stated policy may be to arrest it. In 1956 Walter Salomon[21], private banker and doughty crusader for liberty, emphasized the failure of the Conservatives to cut public expenditure by £100 million, promised by Mr Macmillan:

With public expenditure out of control, a crippling burden of taxes is the natural result . . . Mr Harold Wilson, then Labour Shadow Chancellor was not far wrong when he pointed to the large and growing industry of tax avoidance, even tax evasion, though he was gravely wrong in pinning the whole odium of this noxious practice on the practitioners. The culprits are the Chancellors who have saddled us with this crippling system.

In 1972 Mr Salomon was to refer[22] to an article in *The Times* which identified a general lack of courage as the main cause of failure to take positive action:

Whichever Government is in power seems to stop short of doing what is vital if Britain is to be saved. There are so many vested interests on every hand. So much of Britain's national expenditure is now considered to be sacrosanct, whether it can be afforded or not. So highly is immediate security valued that neither bold adventure nor necessary discomfort can be countenanced to secure it long-term. Britain has become a rigid state.

The situation has changed only for the worse since then.

The maximized freedom of choice which allows, indeed draws the seller and the buyer into the market will involve a full share of mistakes but it will not destroy incentive and it will not centralize power. For where power is diffused (not one boss but a variety of bosses), men are not as a general rule frozen to death in pursuit of competitive enterprise.

At the heart of Marxist Socialism is a stupendous contempt for the individuality of people yet an almost religious elevation of The People. We have only touched on the crimes committed in the name of Socialism, but precisely because it claims to be above the common selfishness of fallible humanity, and because it has a doctrine to which the facts, unwilling peasants, or unfulfillable quotas, have to be reconciled, it can justify as a means to that end, such acts as common, selfish, fallible, market-minded humanity would never even have thought possible.

However, to end on a cheerful note, there have been many historical examples of where man has learnt the lessons of liberty and has actually managed to reverse impending and apparently inevitable economic or political disaster by maximizing instead of minimizing choice. On each occasion deliberately increased choice has led to a striking increase in overall prosperity.

For instance Urukagina of Lagash, who ruled Sumer from about 2350 BC found himself heir to an obnoxious and tyrannical bureaucracy practised by the previous ruler and his palace coterie. High taxation, confiscation of property, every conceivable infringement of personal rights and minimized individual choice were the order of the day. Urukagina introduced the word 'freedom' for the first time in man's recorded history.[23] He brought in sweeping reforms to maximize choice and established a rule of law that protected the rights of individuals however humble, and prevented the abuse of power however elevated. He swept away the oppressive bureaucracy, established honest weights and measures, including a reformed currency.

In the words of his contemporary chroniclers, whereas before the advent of Urukagina, 'the rich, the big men, and the supervisors were getting richer and richer at the expense of the less fortunate citizens, while from one end of the land to the other there were the tax collectors,' after his reforms 'from one end of the land to the other . . . there were no tax collectors.'

But perhaps the most fascinating example of all is the economic miracle wrought by Dr Ludwig Erhard, the German Chancellor, in 1948 when Germany was in a state of economic collapse. Inflation had paralysed industry and commerce. Postwar reconstruction had ground to a standstill and morale was back to its 1945 level.

The population of the western portion, only half the size of pre-war Germany was supporting the added burden of twelve million refugees. Although other West European countries were starting to recover rapidly by 1947, in 1948 German industrial production was still only half the 1936 level, exports were a tenth, and imports a quarter of the 1938 level. Infant mortality was high and food consumption low.[24] The economy was enveloped by a network of price and wage controls intended to offset the effects of the substantial monetary expansion of the war. Because prices were artificially low and there were few enough goods, black markets flourished. In Erhard's words the economy 'had returned to a state of primitive barter'.[25]

The Morgenthau Plan[26] envisaged the move of ten million workers from industry to agriculture and the Potsdam Declaration advocated the restriction of industrial output to 45% below the 1936 level, although this was later increased to match the 1936 level. The aim was to reduce the country to a permanent rural state and it was widely considered that Germany would and should never recover her economic power.

In July 1948, literally 'at a stroke' Dr Erhard introduced his radical economic reforms. Inflated Reichsmarks were replaced with a smaller supply of Deutschmarks. Hundreds of decrees promulgating controls were thrown into the wastepaper basket.

The black market disappeared, shop windows were full of goods, factory chimneys were smoking and the streets swarmed with lorries. . . . On the eve of currency reform, the Germans were aimlessly wandering about their towns searching for a few additional items of food. A day later they thought of nothing but producing them. One day apathy was mirrored on their faces, while on the next the whole nation looked hopefully into the future.[27]

The trade unions, however, called for a general strike, and the civil service began secretly drafting new decrees to re-establish controls. Socialist economists such as Lord (then Doctor) Balogh denounced the Erhard miracle as 'savage deflation . . . which had beggared the middle classes and the workers and irredeemably intensified the instability of the German social system.' He predicted its failure.[28]

However by 1956, Balogh was commending the German example to the British Conservative Government and by 1960 he was to claim that Germany had established itself as the unchallenged economic leader in Europe.[29] He could scarcely do otherwise for the results are outstanding. Between 1950 and 1955 Germany invested more than twice as much as Britain. Real wages in England rose by 12·3% as against 24% in US and 39% in Germany.[30] German exports trebled, incomes doubled and the cost of living rose by only 14% between 1949 and 1956.[31] By 1960 in Germany, France and Japan the improvement in workers' earnings and social benefits was two to three times as high as in Britain.

The real lesson to be drawn from Dr Erhard's success is well summarized by the economist Wilhelm Ropke.[32]

Now there is much talk about the German miracle. For the economist there is no miracle. It is a very simple story of ending economic paralysis and disorder brought about by planning and inflation, and ending it by sound economic order based on two things. First, the freedom of goods and markets, and second on discipline in the field of money . . . the idea was simple. The difficult thing was to put it into practice . . . the miracle was that this return to wisdom and common sense was possible on the political and social levels at a time in which collectivism and inflationism seemed to be triumphant. This had been the essence of National and Socialist economic policy during the Third Reich. . . . It might be almost amusing today to collect all the wrong prophecies and desperate theories which have been invented in order to disprove the striking evidence of the German experiment . . . the Socialists, if they do not want to be defeated in the elections, have to assure that they believe in the market economy and a sound currency . . . so economic law has triumphed over Karl Marx.

The concept is simple, as are most good ideas. The difficulty lies in putting it into practice. That requires courage. Let us hope that our politicians today can find the necessary will and common sense to enable enterprise to flourish once again in a country whose enterprise once led the world.

1   Hobbes: *Leviathan*
2   Jasper Ridley: *Lord Palmerston*, Constable, p. 19
3   Fernand Braudel: *Capitalism and Material Life*, Collins/Fontana, p. 39
4   Ibid. p. 40
5   Ibid. p. 42
6   Ibid. p. 41
7   J. L. and Barbara Hammond: *The Village Labourer 1760–1832* (USA), p. 148, cited in W. Baring Pemberton: *William Cobbett*, Penguin, p. 95
8   S. von Waltershausen: *Deutsche Wirtschaftsgeschichte, 1815–1914*, Fischer 1920, pp. 364 and 372–4, cited in Peter Gay: *The Dilemma of Democratic Socialism*, p. 128

9   Daniel Defoe: *A Tour Through the Whole Island of Great Britain* (1723) Penguin edition, p. 544
10 W. W. Rostow: 'Investment and Real Wages' in *Economic History Review*, May 1938
11 T. S. Ashton: *The Industrial Revolution*, Oxford University Press, pp. 95–7
12 S. Fabricant: *The Output of Manufacturing Industries 1899–1937*, New York, 1940, p. 89. Cited by W. W. Rostow: *The Stages of Economic Growth*, Oxford University Press 1960, p. 89
13 Peter Wiles: 'Top Incomes in the USSR' in *Survey*, Vol. 21, no. 3, 1975
14 Cited by Z. A. B. Zeman: *Prague Spring*, Penguin 1969
15 Robert Conquest: *The Great Terror*, Macmillan 1968; Pelican edition, pp. 48–9
16 Dmitri Vitkovski: *Half a Lifetime*, cited by Alexander Solzhenitsyn in *Gulag Archipelago*, Vol. 2, Collins/Harvill 1975, Fontana edition, p. 91
17 Terry Coleman: *The Navvies*, Penguin
18 Ivan Stadnyuk: 'People are not Angels', *Neva*, Issue 12, 1962, cited by Conquest in *The Great Terror*, p. 46
19 Leonard Schapiro: *The Communist Party of the Soviet Union*, Eyre and Spottiswoode 1960, pp. 454–7
20 Ibid. p. 458
21 W. H. Salomon: *One Man's View*, Churchill Press, p. 52
22 Ibid. p. 53
23 Professor S. N. Kramer: *From the Tablets of Sumer*, USA 1956 and *The Sumerians*, USA 1963
24 W. H. Chamberlain: *The German Phoenix*, Hale 1963, Chapter 2
25 Ludwig Erhard: *Prosperity through Competition*, Thames and Hudson 1958, p. 12
26 H. Morgenthau: *Germany is our Problem*, USA 1945
27 Erhard: op. cit. pp. 10, 11, 13
28 Lord Balogh: *Germany, an Experiment in Planning by the Free Price Mechanism*, Blackwell 1950
29 G. D. N. Worswick (ed.): *Free Trade Proposals*, Blackwell 1960
30 *New Statesman*, 1 December 1956, 19 November 1957
31 Erhard: op. cit. pp. 52, 69, 184, 228, 246
32 Wilhelm Ropke: 'Will West Germany's Free Enterprise System Survive?' in *Commercial & Financial Chronicle*, New York 14 June 1962

Dr Stephen Haseler

Freedom and the Trade Unions

That 'free trade unions are an essential part of a free society' may seem little more than a platitude. It is nevertheless worth emphasizing at the outset of an essay that will be severely critical of modern British trade union practice that the original aims and organization of trade unions are part of our free western heritage. Voluntary associations of workers as collective bargaining units within a free or mixed economy were not only inevitable; but were also understandable. They have provided working men and women with bargaining organizations which have both enhanced their dignity and limited the excesses of the unbalanced capitalist system prevalent at the turn of the century.

A case can be made out that trade unions have also enhanced their members' material welfare as well. Even so, this may be a somewhat exaggerated view. Looked at historically, the momentous rise in the living standards of working people during the course of the twentieth century is more a product of the wealth-generation of the predominantly private ownership system, and of the social reformers who engineered a degree of redistribution within that system, than it is of trade union bureaucrats whose restrictive practice mentality has limited rather than expanded wealth-generation. Trade unions, in this sense, are essentially late nineteenth-century institutions responding to the problems of eighty years ago in a late twentieth-century society. To the extent that they put a check upon modernity and inculcate old class tribalisms they positively hinder economic growth and development—the very seed-corn of working-class affluence in the future. But even if the achievement of trade unions in enhancing their members' welfare, both in the past and for the future, is questionable, what certainly is not at issue is their major role in acting as buffers between the individual and the state. Autonomous intermediary institutions are vital for a free society. Indeed they are part of the definition of a free system, and are absent in all totalitarian states.

Free trade unions, at least as we understand them in the West, were originally conceived of as voluntary organizations for the specific purpose of looking after the economic interests of the workers. With the weakening of the traditional social ties of family, kinship, community and religion by industrialism and mass democracy, free trade unions became a valuable social institution which, together with other intermediate institutions, can help to limit the power of the State. They can be part of a pattern of organizations which help to diffuse the concentration of power. As the United Kingdom does not possess federal political systems or a particularly effective separation of powers at central level then, in our unitary, centralized State the trade unions should, theoretically at least, represent a check upon all-embracing State power.

Unfortunately, in recent years trade union leaders, instead of resisting the growth of the State have become conscious agents for its expansion, and following its increasing all-pervasiveness they have wanted a share in the power of the new Leviathan. Increasingly, British trade union leaders have removed themselves from their historic function and become the bosses themselves. They are present on all manner of boards, commissions and government agencies. Both formally and informally, they help to determine government policy and run the State. They have, in short, and voluntarily, become agents of the State; a State they do not oppose when necessary on behalf of their members but rather a State in which they feel at home in the upper reaches and which they want to see even further expanded.

Some trade union leaders want not only to become enmeshed in an ever-expanding state, but also want to destroy free trade unionism by turning trade union representatives into employers.

The Bullock proposals[1] for industrial democracy, published in 1977, foresee for trade unionists at all levels a totally new role, a function unwanted by a previous generation of trade unionists. The Bullock Committee wants trade unionists on the board of medium-sized and large companies. It also suggests that the method whereby employees should arrive on the board should be exclusively through the trade union route. Hence trade union officials become, at one and the same time, employees and employers—a dual role which blurs the proper functions of both management and unions. It leads, inevitably, to the use of irresponsible power. 'Irresponsible' because no one has, or need take, responsibility for their actions.

Both in relation to the State and to private and public enterprises we therefore are witnessing a total reversal of the traditional role of trade unions. The scholar will rightly ask: how has all this come about? How is it that voluntary associations of workers, with the duty to protect their members' interests against both the State and the private employers, have become themselves both part of the State and potentially part of the management? How can it be that such a revolutionary change in function can have been engineered in such a short period of time?

The answers to these questions are essentially three-fold. First, it is crucial to an understanding of this revolutionary process to grasp the modern fact of the sheer power of organized labour. As society and the economy has become more industrialized and collectivized, so the institutions of organized labour, not necessarily the individual worker, have become—almost by natural process—more capable of halting or paralysing the industrial process. This is particularly so in nations such as Britain with a large working class. Just as Britain is arguably the most 'proletarian' society in the West, so also it is the country with the most powerful unions.

In a highly complex industrial society, with many inter-linked processes, even small groups of workers—if they are strategically placed—can bring massive power to bear upon society as a whole. Power workers, for instance, can by withdrawing their labour bring to a standstill essential public services within hours of their taking industrial action. Dockers can stop imports, train drivers and truckers can curtail the distribution of food.

Of course, this has always been the case since the emergence of the modern economy. Yet only in recent years has it become obvious to the general public. The sheer political and industrial power of organized labour has probably only been perceived as a distant threat, pushed back into the recesses of the mind, until the Heath government of the early seventies. What has brought organized labour's full potential to the fore of all our minds was the confrontation between the miners and Heath which was carried on between 1971 and 1974, a contest which the miners, in reality and in the full glare of national and international publicity, essentially won. It was following 1974 that sheer panic spread through the British political establishment and a 'Social Contract' was formed as a means of ameliorating the tension in the situation and as a means of giving people time to think about what had happened. Once an elected government had so publicly and obviously been humbled by a powerful union it could no longer be plausibly argued that the British lived under the sort of representative democracy, based upon the sovereignty of Parliament, that the textbooks claimed. What had been feared for some time by only the perceptive became the all too often proclaimed reality—'no government can run the country without the co-operation of the trade unions'. And co-operation was often a synonym for agreement or submission.

If the early seventies in Britain represented the historical point at which the always latent power of organized labour actually made itself publicly felt, then it was also the period when the authority of the Parliamentary State was seen to crumble. In fact, the progressive weakening of the authority (not the all-pervasiveness—that is different) of the State is the second reason for the emergence of over-mighty trade union power.

Since the emergence of mass democracy during the early part of the twentieth century and right up until the seventies the peoples of the United Kingdom could properly argue that they lived under a system of Parliamentary government and the rule of law. The State possessed both authority and legitimacy. Parliament ruled. Its laws were obeyed by all the various pressure and interest groups within the nation. There was a political consensus behind Parliamentary government. People thought, by and large, that voting counted and that elected politicians governed the broad direction of our society. Although there was public anxiety about the power of some of the vested interests it would have been unlikely that an opinion poll taken in the fifties or even in the early sixties would have revealed the British people as believing that a trade union leader was more powerful than the elected Prime Minister.

Also, the Labour movement in its widest sense (party, unions and co-operatives) did not historically set itself against the Parliamentary state. Indeed it was wedded to the social-democratic tradition (or at least its leaders were) that the life of Labour was essentially subordinate to the wider loyalty that was owed to the nation and its political institutions.

Yet, over the years the authority of the State has seemed to wane. As it has become more intrusive, as it enters areas of life in which it is either unwanted or incompetent, then its allure, and with it the allure of those who run it, begins to fade. Together with this poverty of authority has gone a draining of the confidence of an erstwhile supremely assured political class. The reasons for this are for another essay—suffice it to say that this collapse in morale has coincided with an increasing awareness of power on the part of the leaders of the new emerging class, the late twentieth-century trade union bureaucrat.

A third, and arguably the most important, factor in accounting for the revolutionary change in the role and power of trade unions in Britain is the changing political characteristics of trade union leaders. Trade union power may have burgeoned naturally with the development of the modern economy. This has gone hand in hand with the dissipation of State authority as its vast apparatus grew. But the added new dimension from the mid sixties onwards in Britain was the 'politicization' from the top of the trade union movement in a direction which was to bring it, inevitably, into conflict with the liberal democratic order.

Trade unions, of course, wield political influence in all Western societies, and there is nothing particularly unhealthy about that. All the large pressure groups should properly have a considerable influence upon democratic governments. Even so, the

British situation is rather different from that of many of our allies. For instance, in the United States the trade union and labour movement is not only less strategically placed to wield political power but has historically represented workers who feel themselves to be an integral part of, and to have a vested interest in the success of capitalism. American trade union leaders— particularly those in power in the American Federation of Labor and Congress of Industrial Organisations—not only determine to make the free enterprise system work but have been extremely critical of their own government's 'detente' policies with the Soviet Union. In many respects they have carried on an alternative foreign policy during the years of 'detente', remaining highly critical of US grain sales to the Soviet Union and providing platforms for leading Soviet dissidents. They seem to understand that the first person to suffer from totalitarianism is the worker.

In Europe too, the trade union situation is somewhat different from that at home. In France and Italy trade unions have historically been divided politically into Communist, Socialist and Christian groups—owing political loyalties across the spectrum. This naturally diffuses both their political objectives and power.

Of the major Western nations it is only in Britain and in West Germany that organized labour is politically united and has the potential for concerted political action. Yet in both these countries the political complexion of the union leaders has, until recently anyway, been firmly aligned to the social-democratic traditions of the major left of centre political party.

It is in Britain that the most revolutionary change has occurred. From the inception of organized labour in the United Kingdom trade union organization has been organically linked to the British Labour Party. Indeed Ernest Bevin was accurate in describing the Labour Party as 'coming out of the bowels of the TUC'. This organizational link has meant that the Labour Party apparatus in the country has been largely financed and controlled by trade unions. At the Annual Conference of the Labour Party the trade unions, through their system of 'bloc votes', cast roughly five-sixths of the votes. This enables them, effectively, to determine the policies of the Labour Party organization. Trade unions also determine the composition of a majority of the members of Labour's National Executive Committee, the body which runs the party in between Annual Conferences.

Trade unions have a more diluted influence upon Labour Members of Parliament, but even so the MPs as a body (the Parliamentary Labour Party) do not like separating themselves over-much from political opinion within the central trade union leadership. Some Labour MPs—about a third—are directly sponsored by trade unions in the sense that the union they represent funds part of their election expenses. These 'sponsored' Members are naturally rather more sensitive than others about trade union opinion. Also, aspiring National Executive Committee members had better not run foul of trade union opinion either.

This organic link between the trade unions and the Labour Party has given British trade union leaders a direct access to politics at the highest level ever since Labour became a major party of State. It is for this reason that Labour's traditional social-democratic leadership had been keen upon ensuring that the leaders of the major trade unions continued to represent the moderate views of their members. Far-sighted leaders of the Labour Party always understood that a left-wing-dominated trade union movement would have immense repercussions both upon the political complexion of Labour itself but also upon the general political balance in the country.

Following World War II in the period of the Attlee government, and during the fifties and early sixties, the leadership of Britain's major trade unions were in the hands of robust defenders of the liberal democratic system. Although Ernest Bevin, the inter-war General Secretary of the Transport and General Workers' Union, was in the government from 1945 to 1950 all the major union leaders broadly shared his view of politics. Communists were banned from holding office in most of the major trade unions and the TUC as an act of policy supported the setting up of NATO and the consequent Western defence posture. The TUC was so suspicious of the motives of the Soviet bloc that it pulled out of The World Federation of Trade Unions after it had become Communist-dominated and set up The International Confederation of Free Trade Unions in alliance with the American union movement. Today there is a constant flow of top British trade union leaders to Eastern Europe and reciprocal visits have been made to the TUC by such figures as Shelepin, the former head of the KGB.

It is not an exaggeration to suggest that the right-wing trade union leaders of the fifties were instrumental in helping to secure the leadership of the Labour Party for Hugh Gaitskell upon the resignation of Clement Attlee in 1955. In other words, the social-democratic men of the fifties had a keen awareness of the need to keep Labour within the system and to resist Communist or Trotskyite penetration of what was even then seen as the most powerful single pressure group within British society. In a very real sense they were securing the very foundations of British democratic society. Once, they argued, the trade unions 'went', then, eventually and inevitably so would 'everything else'.

Of course, the left within the Labour movement saw it this way as well. The Communist Party of Great Britain had no electoral support whatsoever, had been rebuffed in their various overtures to Labour for affiliation or for 'Popular Frontism', and consequently could only make headway within British politics by attempting to gain control of key trade unions. This was also the aim of other left groups, principally the embryonic 'Tribune' left which was the successor to the 'Bevanite' group of the late forties and early fifties.

Very little headway was made by the left until the middle sixties. Then, all of a sudden, it all changed. The two most powerful unions, the TGWU and the AEU (as it then was) slipped from right to left-wing control. Jack Jones, an extreme leftist, became General-Secretary of the Transport Union and Hugh Scanlon, of similar political persuasion, became President of the Engineers' within a year of each other. Other unions also began to change their political complexion—the single most important being the National Union of Mineworkers, which was to play such a crucial role in later battles with the Heath government.[2]

This rather dramatic shift at the top of some of the major

unions towards the left allowed the Communist Party opportunities that were denied to it by the earlier generation of
social-democratic leaders. Always present at local, regional and
national level, the Communist trade union apparatus could now
more easily push forward its influence. They remained faithful
to the advice Lenin gave them at the foundation of the British
Communist Party in 1920:

We must be able to make any sacrifice, and even if need be . . . resort to
various stratagems, artifices and illegal methods, to evasions and sub-
terfuges, as long as we can get into the trade unions, remain in them,
and carry on communist work within them at all costs.[3]

With the major barrier of anti-Communist unionism removed,
the Communist Party expanded its influence quite rapidly
within the structures of most of Britain's trade unions. They
were not, however, the only extreme left group at work. The
increasing politicization of British trade unionism also went
hand in hand, particularly as the British economy entered into
periods of high inflation and unemployment, with a radical-
ization of the shop stewards' movement. The British industrial
base is now peopled—at active level—by thousands of shop
stewards whose aims are political and not industrial. Concern for
the betterment of wages and conditions has given way in many
cases to the use of every conceivable industrial grievance to
'smash the system'—the system being the mixed pluralistic
economy.

Communists and the various Trotskyite groups do not necessarily always agree on methods and tactics, and they also have
constant ideological quarrels. Communists are usually more
careful and serious and less sloganistic in their approach to industrial disputes than are the ultra-left. There is also a debate
both between Communists and Trotskyites and within the Communist Party about attitudes towards the Soviet Union. Even so,
they all share one common aim—the overthrow of capitalism
and the liberal, democratic system and its replacement by some
form of 'Socialist State'. It is important to understand that to
them trade unions are a method, a mechanism, for the achievement of a totally new political order. They are not perceived as a

purely social or industrial organization.

It is hardly surprising, therefore, that with the increasingly strategically placed power of organized labour in society allied to a weakened authority of the over-blown state and the 'politicization' of trade union bureaucracies that trade unions should assume a directly political role.

This manifests itself in an increasing number of political strikes. Even though Marxists understand all strikes as political, as each industrial dispute increases the 'workers' understanding of the class nature of the struggle', some are more overtly so than others. It was during the Heath government that spectacular displays of industrial action or threats of industrial action for political purposes were an almost constant feature of daily life. For instance, the threatened one-day general strike called by the TUC to release five dockers gaoled by the Industrial Relations Court in 1972 was unashamedly political in character. So was the threatened AUEW strike in 1974 over its refusal to pay fines, damages and costs imposed by the same court—a court set up by a duly elected Parliament upon the basis of a manifesto pledge made by the victorious party in the previous general election. Both these threats were attempts to interfere, by industrial means, in the judicial process. The one-day 'general strike' in 1973, euphemistically termed 'a national day of protest and stoppage' called by the TUC against wage control policy was an attempt by organized labour leaderships to undermine and challenge Parliamentary authority. Whatever the merits of a prices and incomes policy—statutorily based—ultimate policy questions in a mature society should be decided by persuasion and voting, not by direct action of this kind.

The other way in which the political nature of trade union leaders asserts itself is through the novel constitutional mechanism of the 'Social Contract'. But underlying this formal and open method of government/trade union leader consultation lies an awesome assumption about modern government: that an elected Parliament has essentially yielded up its ultimate responsibility to an extra-Parliamentary body which can exercise a veto over major policy questions. During the negotiations for an International Monetary Fund loan in the autumn of 1976, the British government was reduced to a runner, or a broker, between the demands of our international creditors and the policies which would be acceptable to the TUC. Trade union leaders, conscious of their power, now act increasingly as politicians. They help to determine budgets, levels of public expenditure and are increasingly drawn into open political warfare between the parties. How else can one describe the statement by Jack Jones, the Transport Workers' leader, that the co-operation of the trade union movement would 'depend on the introduction of Socialist policies'.[4]

So powerful have the leaders of organized labour apparently become that the central political issue of our times in Britain has become: can a Conservative government govern? Can any government, elected by popular mandate, effectively control policy if it is opposed by the TUC?

That such a question can actually be asked is itself a measure of the extent to which Britain has already entered a form of post-democracy. For even to ask these questions is to half-admit that popular representative democracy no longer in fact functions. The people, through a free and secret ballot, may choose a government but in reality that choice is being rendered worthless. If the people choose wrongly then they will be over-ruled.

How then can a responsible democratic society so order its affairs that the trend to extra-Parliamentary trade union power of recent years can be reversed? How can we both recognize the legitimate power of trade unions and curb their excesses? How can we de-politicize union leaders so as to return the primary political responsibility to elected representatives?

It is always difficult to reverse a trend. Once a new class has tasted power it can be a shattering experience to wrest power back from them. However, the argument for doing so is sound and is based upon our liberal, democratic Western political heritage. Essentially it is up to politicians, democratic politicians, to give voice to it and by their resolution so re-fashion our present political system as to return power to the people. Politicians can, however, hardly be expected to re-shape the economy so that unions can no longer possess such a strategic control over the industrial process. But they can revivify the authority of the Parliamentary State to the point where most citizens at least understand the difference between industrial action for limited purposes and political action disguised as trade union practice.

It surely cannot be beyond the wit of politicians, even our present generation, to spell out fearlessly and if need be provocatively, the proper responsibilities of free trade unions in a democratic society. The sheer majesty of the electoral process has to be re-affirmed as the primary decision-making process, and trade union leaders relegated in the psychology and atmospherics of political life to the position of important, but *not* pre-eminent, interest group bargainers. This simple educational process can hardly begin whilst politicians of all parties continue to fail, become unpopular and consequently lower the esteem of Parliament in the process. As Parliament, and politicians, become increasingly the objects of derision—because of failure, corruption, insensitivity and inability to communicate—then the revivification of the State becomes impossible and ordinary people will continue to turn to other organized bodies for protection, be it the Scottish National Party or the trade unions or other sectional groupings. In short, in order for democratic politicians properly to confront trade union power they must first of all become successful. A democratic society has a vested interest in success. The awesome fact has to be faced that whilst general economic, social and international failure continues to cling to our political representatives they will never be a match for the trade union barons.

Although the revival of Parliamentary institutions may be difficult, the de-politicization of trade union officials will be easier. The fact remains that the vast majority of ordinary workers do not share the extremist political sympathies of their shop stewards, and their regional and national officials. Communist, Trotskyite or Marxist officials attain power amongst a workforce which is one-third Tory and two-thirds social-democratic in political outlook simply because of the byzantine, archaic and often secretive structures of trade union decision-making processes. A compulsory postal ballot, enforced by law, for all national, regional and branch officials would ensure a more politically representative trade union leadership. There is no reason either why a statute should not insist upon the regular election of top officials of trade unions. It is laughable for trade unions to insist that they are democratically organized whilst the largest union in the country elects its General-Secretary 'for life' (that is, until retirement age).

The only other major area for legislative involvement should be in the admittedly sensitive area of the 'closed shop'. If trade unions are to be voluntary associations of workers which bargain collectively for their best interests, then the *compulsion* involved in the 'closed shop' must be outlawed. Workers must be free, not only to choose their leaders, but to leave their unions and form new ones if they feel that their unions are not properly representing them.

Both the postal ballot and the ability to form new unions will give the worker greater power not less. The freedom to change officials without having to sit through endless branch meetings, often until midnight, and the freedom to leave one union and help form another without getting the sack will frighten the life out of the present generation of comfortable, reactionary, cocooned, left-wing trade union bureaucrats. They will have to justify their existence by supplying a need. Workers will cease being the pawns in a political struggle and assume a new dignity at work.

None of this will, necessarily, guarantee less industrial militancy, nor should it. The best trade union official will be the one who can get the best deal for his members without putting them out of work by raising prices excessively. In short, the trade union leader will have to assume the responsibility for his actions. He or she will have to take into account the economic position of the firm or plant or nationalized industry or government enterprise before a claim is made. If the trade union leader gets it wrong then there should be no automatic assumption that he or she can remain in the job for ever. Nor should there be an assumption that a union which continues to misrepresent its members should continue for ever. Officials and unions should be able to come and go according to results.

This may all sound rather revolutionary, particularly in the complacent (though declining) restrictive-practice-laden world of Britain in the late seventies. Even so, the original aim of trade union organization was to give to workers by hand and by brain a dignity and a choice which was denied to them by an earlier excessively unbalanced capitalism. Trade unions were brought into being also to improve the wages and conditions of their members, not to rule over them in perpetuity like some new boss class.

We must ensure that modern trade union bureaucrats are taken off the backs of the workers, that they are responsible for their actions and that they leave - ultimate political decision-making to those whom *all* the workers elect through Parliamentary democratic institutions.

1 Cmd 6706
2 Most of the senior figures of the General Council of the TUC had, by the middle of 1977, contributed articles to the Communist Party newspaper, the *Morning Star*. This in itself may signify little more than political open-mindedness. However, if leading Conservative politicians contributed articles to the newspaper of the National Front, decent political opinion would be outraged.
3 V. I. Lenin: *Selected Works*, Vol. 3, pp. 318–19 (Progress Publishers, Moscow)
4 *Panorama* (BBC television) interview by Michael Charlton with Jack Jones, Monday 3 May 1976

Norris McWhirter

Freedom of Choice

If the time span of the existence of *Homo sapiens* is likened to a single year, 'choice' is something which appeared late in the afternoon of 31 December. Choice is the product of civilization. Since history has been written over a period of five and a half millenia, eighteen of our twenty-six recorded civilizations have collapsed. The freedom of choice can exist only during part of the life-cycle of a civilization. It is a barometer of its health.

Since freedom of choice is something interwoven with the fortunes of any civilization, a look at their ups and downs deserves some study. At the start of the twentieth century Western civilization dominated the world. It was epitomized by the Empires of Britain, France and Germany and to a lesser extent those of Spain, Portugal and Tsarist Russia. Additionally, the youthful USA which was without imperial tradition was beginning to outstrip Western Europe economically.

By comparison the rest of the world's surviving civilizations—the Far Eastern, the Hindu, the two orthodox Christian civilizations under Tsarism (Eastern and Muscovite) and the two Islamic civilizations (Arabic and Iranic) were sickly. Since then the mainstream of Far Eastern civilization became submerged in Maoism in 1949 with only South Korea and Japan still engaging in free enterprise economies. The Orthodox Christian culture after ten centuries began to be rigorously repressed in the Soviet Union from 1917 but has still between thirty and fifty million courageous adherents trying to exercise the freedom of religious worship. Both the Islamic civilizations, which were fast fading, received a transfusion in the fifties from the exploitation of oil and have shown generally a continued resistance to the Communist credo.

Because the very word 'civilize' has the sense of 'reclaiming from barbarism', modern historians balk at the categorizing of the highly imperialist Communist civilization as the world's twenty-sixth and hence the arch rival of what is chronologically the world's eighteenth—the Western civilization. This however is a misunderstanding of the criteria of a civilization. A civilization is not merely a common cultural condition but a separate imperialist design. That the Soviet Union shares some technology and music with the West is of small consequence. The fact that the Kremlin has never relinquished its declared aim of world domination is what distinguishes it. To those who still feel that a system, which in two generations showed the inside of labour camps to an estimated 66,000,000 people, cannot be labelled as a civilization one has to recall other historical facts. Roman civilization officially encouraged or tolerated the fiendish cruelty of gladiatorial combat for seven centuries while for three and a half centuries between 1518 and 1865 an estimated 1·8 million Africans died being assembled by their fellow Africans and in transit and disposal by Arab and Western slavers.

In all matters of individual freedom and in the exercise of personal choice it is a prerequisite to understand the nature of the conflict between the old Western civilization and the new Communist civilization. It is the aim of the new to destroy the old. It is the aim of the old to tame and absorb the young. What, however, is crystallizing after sixty years is not purely an internal struggle within each of the sovereign states.

In the West the internal struggle is that between the libertarian elements and the corporatists. The nationalizers, the neo-Keynesians and the advocates of universal welfare with their cohorts of index-pensioned civil servants are ranged against the advocates of market economics, non-State education and private enterprise on whose very effort and endeavour the former feed.

In the occupied Eastern bloc countries human rights campaigners, now dubbed 'dissidents', carry on their extraordinarily courageous and one-sided struggle against the mighty *apparatchiki* and disinformation agencies of a politically totalitarian state.

In the internal struggle within as yet non-Communist countries, Britain has led the way towards corporatism *via* the Webbs, Russell, Cole, Laski, Keynes, Beveridge, Titmuss, Attlee, Wilson, Benn *et al.* Contrariwise the Soviet Union has thrown up (and out) the foremost apostles of individual freedom Solzhenitsyn and Bukovsky.

It is against this wider canvas of conflicting ideologies, each claiming the monopoly of true human compassion, that we have here to examine the three major facets of the freedom of choice—taxation, national health and education.

Taxation has an immensely long history as an institution. Its imposition is recorded as early as the earliest of all civilizations in Sumer. Great nation states of the past have been broken merely by bad taxation systems—by bad is meant inequitable, inefficient, overcomplicated and/or inconsistent. Great Britain is however now in an advanced state of national decline largely due to the ever-mounting weight of a highly complex taxation system which has been laid on her population in annual layers. Systems which strive to achieve 'absolute' fairness end up being incomprehensible.

In a democracy, in which the electoral power of a man who draws £80 a week from Social Security is identical to that of a man who lone-handed earns £800 a week in overseas currency, policies of short-sighted egalitarianism are provenly irresistible to the cynical politician. In the same way that there are ironmongers, fishmongers and costermongers so politicians are essentially votemongers. They trade in power and the more threatened the withdrawal of that power the more unprincipled they become in legislating to retain it. This process is the more nauseous because the process is obscured by the cloying sanctity of the Robin Hood syndrome. The fact is that taxation at even half the present (1978) levels can only deter enterprise, destroy incentive and savings and encourage emigration of the skilled.

Up until the nineteenth century the aspirant for a seat in Parliament could send his agent round the few dozen eligible voters in his constituency with a small bag of golden guineas or, after 1816, golden sovereigns. With the march towards universal franchise finally attained in 1928, because of the sheer numbers involved, electoral bribery became not only enforcibly illegal but financially impracticable. Politicians thus had to resort to electoral bribery by using other people's money by a process of legalized confiscation. The process of transference of resources from private to governmental (meaning party political) hands is a transfer from a more economic to a less and less economic use. It is thus both impoverishing and collectively inhumane.

This inexorable and debilitating process has proceeded with Fabian stealth on the lobster-pot principle. Those to be taxed in ever-increasing (known as 'progressive') amounts are not thrown into the boiling water. Rather they are rendered lethargic and finally insensible by being brought slowly to precisely that same ultimate temperature with only a murmur rather than a scream. Some measure of how this process has been developed by a party political system and its acolytes, who know not knight starvation, can be shown in the table overleaf.

In the three decades of post-war Britain there has been a consistent policy of corporatism—the macro-economic approach epitomized by high taxation, universal welfare, centralized planning, state control, high public spending, massive bureaucracy, income and price policies, trade unions with legal immunities and ever diminishing individual freedom. The alternative of low taxation, selective welfare, decentralized planning, limited government, essential public expenditure, small bureaucracy, free wage negotiation, market force pricing, non-monopoly trade unions subject to democratic secret ballot and increasing personal freedom is attainable only if there is the zest, zeal and motive to attain it.

The last thirty years are an inheritance from Lord Keynes, advocate of State-generated demand, 'full employment' and hence father of budget deficit spending thus leading inevitably to wage and price inflation and recurrent balance of payments

crises. His disciple R. M. Titmuss kept up the deadly work of
dishonest money supported by such third-generation thinkers
as Professor Brian Abel Smith of the LSE, author of *People
Without Choice*, and Professor Peter Townsend the sociologist
pro vice-chancellor of Essex University and formerly of PEP
(Political and Economic Planning).

United Kingdom—Growth in Total Taxation
Central Statistical Office data

Year		Total Taxation in £ (millions)	% of Gross National Product taken
1913–14	Pre World War I	£250	10%
1930–31	Slump Year	£960	21%
1938–39	Reluctant Rearmament	£1,220	23%
1946–47	Year of Nationalization	£3,490	39%
1960–61	After 3 successive Tory won General Elections	£7,350	32%
1965–66	First Wilson Budget	£11,140	35%
1970–71	First Heath Budget	£19,110	48%
1976–77	First Callaghan Budget	£31,197	59%

Note: Column 1 is current values hence contorted by high inflation rates
and therefore of no *comparative* value. Column 2 however being a ratio
demonstrates the real trend.

The table is a barometer of the ratchet-like advance of collectivism under which successive governments have advanced
'social welfare' by ever further restricting the freedom of
producers, traders, property-owners, investors and consumers
who, wearing other hats, are themselves recipients of welfare.
The process has been promoted on the basis that it is the only

compassionate answer to the 'problem' of securing Beveridge's freedoms from 'want, idleness, disease and squalor'. In the thirties a sizeable minority of our populations were afflicted by one or more of these inhumanities but by sleight of hand the vote-mongers have not made the welfare of such minorities the prime concern of the Welfare State at all. Their Welfare State for electoral reasons was constructed *from the outset* to be a pot into which all had to put in and from which all should also be able to take out. It was, in the words of Arthur Shenfield, 'a scheme not for steering welfare to the needy but for a nationalizing welfare for all'.

The myth that you cannot have welfare without a Welfare State is assiduously cultivated by the army of civil servants. Their concern for the long term public good *must* be coloured by their short term personal concern in building career structures and retiring on elevated pensionable grades. The truth of course is that you can only supply effective welfare to the really needy by *not* having a largely indiscriminate 'universal' entitlement to welfare. The abandonment of the sacred 'principle of universality' would however not merely undermine the politically essential element of electoral bribery with other people's earnings but would open the door to something far more fundamental—denationalization of welfare. The old argument about the administrative difficulty of having selective (and effective) welfare fell to the ground with the advent of the computer a quarter of a century ago.

In any economically healthy society the welfare of the small minority of really needy would be well within the compass of private enterprise institutions. A free market as opposed to a monopoly in welfare could not fail to produce results so spectacularly better in value that beneficiaries would *really* benefit. If welfare were confined to the really needy and the rest were free to make their own arrangements in a competitive market, humanity would really be served. The tax money saved would be applied far more to the general good of the national economy if left in the hands of the taxpayers.

Modern politicians however are not deflected by such unpalatable commonplaces and continue to feed on the reassurance from State-paid ideologues, sociologists and academics. The problem with people who claim to be the monopolists of human compassion is that they soon actually believe in their own claim. It is one of the hazards of public life that those in it by continually meeting people with a common aim thereby reinforce their delusions.

Next to Social Security and Pensions the two next most massive calls on Public Expenditure are Education and Health. One of the truths which compulsory state education has carefully failed to teach its customers in its 106 years is that all governments are not only fallible but of themselves penniless. The concept that 'the Government' has its *own* bottomless purse is a myth useful to collectivists. It is nurtured by 'social engineers' who seek to advance their pleadings and legislate in a way that is irreversible and non-justiciable.

The cutting of public expenditure to revive dynamism in the economy presents a problem akin to that of weaning already drug-dependent individuals back to health. Virtually two whole generations have now had their self-reliance sapped. They are 'hooked' on 'free' handouts to the long predictable point that any turning off of the tap would quite possibly lead to violent withdrawal symptoms. In a Fabian world lobster-pots can be allowed to cool slowly too. In fact if debt interest is properly allowed for the total budgeted cost of the 1979/80 welfare programme, so far from representing the trumpeted decrease over 1976/7 levels at 1975 prices, represented an *increase!* The collectivist's definition of a public spending cut is a reduction in the size of the originally planned increase. Professor Donnison of the Supplementary Benefit Commission has publicly extolled the higher morality of extra-budgetary spending. .

The National Health Scheme (NHS) was introduced in the United Kingdom in 1949 amid paeons of praise and a quite sincere glow of righteousness. Here was a scheme that was 'the envy of the world'. Though imitation is said to be the sincerest form of flattery, after nearly thirty years no other major country has in fact remotely copied it.

The laudable socialist theory behind the NHS was that the nation's health would rapidly improve through free preventive medicine to the point that expenditure would decline. Preventive unlike curative medicine cannot however be imposed and today constitutes a very small proportion of the vast total expenditure. The increase in expectation of life is in some quarters claimed as a triumph of socialized medicine. It is something for which credit might be more justly claimed by sanitary engineers and entrepreneurial pharmacology than by a hopelessly bureaucratized NHS.

The fundamental problem of the NHS is one of the several ineluctible laws of economics—namely that if the price of any valuable service (medical attention) is nil then the demand for it rises to the point that the supply of it has to be suppressed. Increasing charges (already 20 per cent in France) may be soon predicted.

When this reaches a certain point anxious former BUPA (British United Provident Association) and PPP (Private Patients Plan) patients will escape in increasing measure to Crown Dependencies, the Irish Republic or should it come about even a devolved Scotland or Wales for treatment by English doctors, who have voted with their feet. If there had been any remaining doubt about the importance of choice in the scheme of priorities among many individuals the survival of private medical insurance provides it. Their clients do not pay twice but thrice—once for the NHS in their taxes, and twice more because their insurance scheme has to be paid out of other income already taxed. Those who rail about the privileged 'rich' jumping the queue overlook the fact that in a bus queue if some desperate person hails a taxi not only does he shorten the queue but he may already have bought his bus season ticket in advance at the bus station.

The declining morale in the National Health Scheme is something which was predictable and inevitable. Anything run as one huge operation by a ministry must suffer from the inefficiency and frustration innate in such a mechanism. Medicine is essentially a hierarchical profession and within it egality or democracy has little scope. The organization of porters and cleaners into powerful unions was bound sooner rather than later to conflict with chain of command and the exercise of professional judgement. The word 'crisis' is not part of the vocabulary of people who work on minutely recorded overtime.

The almost pathological hatred of 'pay-beds' of those who have a low threshold of envy spilled over in 1975. Their excision from the system became in that year ministerial policy. By 1977 it was clear that the urgency with which they were to be phased out was based on political expediency rather than clinical common sense. The fact that tens of millions of pounds were being lost mattered little.

The repercussions of the attack on the 'impurity' of a private sector within a socialized scheme are profoundly damaging to the scheme. Predictably more and more young and newly qualified doctors are taking double-banked examinations to enable them to cut and run to any other country where choice and liberty counts for as much as egality. The removal of the irritant of an elitism within curative and preventive medicine has led to a destructive lowering of standards. The high fliers are flying out with one-way tickets. Self advancement and self interest may not be the most noble of human instincts but it is provenly unsafe to underestimate their strength. Your true egalitarian would always prefer to have a morass of mediocrity rather than vestigial pinnacles of privilege. Your true humanitarian would only seek to curb excesses of inequality. To eliminate inequality runs counter to incentive and motivation without which no profession can deliver. Some major benefits can only accrue to those entire communities in which personal priority of personal expenditure remains permissible.

One should not leave the matter of freedom in medicine without some comment on medicine in North America. The running there of perhaps the world's most efficient medical monopoly at ruinous cost to the consumer is God's gift to those who are not slow to confuse non-State enterprise with free enterprise.

If emotion runs high in the field of health, it must run even higher in education. The numbers are larger, embracing all the healthy as well as the unhealthy. Those being treated are the young and the impressionable at the outset of life rather than those at its tail end. Education can be concerned not merely with maximizing the potential of the mind but also with the manipulation of the heart by one-sided indoctrination.

In Britain in the post-war era the elimination of non-State education and the elimination of selection of any kind have been the kernel of debate. The ultimate aim of the egalitarian has been obscured by their step-by-step ratchet approach. The fact that there can be a political educational policy at all is because of one fact. The supply of education has become a virtual state monopoly—at least $93\frac{1}{2}\%$ nationalized. The inherent dangers in such a system are manifold. If an all-pervasive policy turns out to be misconceived then that entire facet of social life is debilitated for a minimum of two generations. Only macro-organisms have the potential for massive damage. Micro-organisms, particularly if they are like apples on racks rather than in barrels, need not transmit their rottenness.

The whole thrust of governmental policy on education has been to ignore the 1944 Education Act's concept that in reality children differ not merely in age but also in aptitude and ability. The greatest censored scientific truth is that all men are born unequal—even identical twins, who are genetically the same person to the point that they can give each other skin grafts, are unequal.

The egalitarians, instead of glorying in the variety and differences within mankind, are overwhelmed by the desire to impose uniformity and conformity. The irony of the situation is that Communist regimes run the most blatant elitism in education anywhere in the world. It is essential to their competitive struggle against the inherently more economically efficient system of capitalism. Thus, while Western democracies emasculate their competitive ability with egalitarian educational policies, those in charge of policy in those countries which so many educationalists seek to emulate run diametrically opposed policies—it is a form of quite deliberate unilateral disarmament in a world in which competitiveness and productivity are the *real politik* of prosperity.

The two most nakedly and blatantly elite educational establishments in the world are probably the Frunze Military Academy in the USSR and the Lenin School outside Havana in Marxist Cuba. The latter creams off the island's top 3% of talent both academic and physical into a hothouse whose products will be unleashed on an unsuspecting world. Whether their highly intensive teaching ratio, lavish equipment, Olympic-sized gymnasium and swimming pool and championship track, impoverish or enrich the other 97% on the island, is something on which their government take a very raw capitalistic view.

The arguments in favour of non-competitive egalitarianism in Britain are not merely destructive of individual freedom but, though made in the name of humanity, will rapidly produce extremely inhumane results for the entire populace. There are already and inevitably reflecting themselves in declining standards of literacy and numeracy. The more apparent this becomes the greater will be the effort to obfuscate the statistics which give proof of it. The identity of the first comprehensive which failed to secure a single 'O' (let alone an 'A') level in a whole academic year is not mentioned in polite educational circles. If professedly and ostensibly well-meaning educationalists obscure the end-product of their disastrous policies then they cease to be in the category of searchers after truth. They move into the category of those whose unrepentant self-indulgence is wanton.

The moral superiority affected by the educationalists of these last fifty years has been based on the contention that those who dissent are unfeeling people without a spark of humanity for the less well endowed. Increasingly it is becoming obvious that so far from being the monopolists of human compassion they are the arrogant architects of the frustration and misery of missed opportunity. Equality of opportunity is their creed but equality of missed opportunity is their practice. Because there is no practical possibility of optimizing the potential for all, there is no arguable case for the doctrine being now practised of optimizing the potential of none.

A milder and more defensible policy would be for parents no longer to be excluded and obstructed in trying to play a parental role. That would require far greater variety of schools than the present 'ministerial circulars' decree. Successive ministers have never sought to have Parliament's will, as expressed by the 1944 Education Act, repealed. Rather they sought to circumvent both its spirit and its letter by the succession of *diktats*. The Curzon Street view has long been that democratically elected councillors on Local Education Authorities can have any form of education they wish provided it is comprehensive. Having virtually 'won' the battle to enforce this system which is only occasionally successful as the universal panacea, the coping stone of the Department of Education and Science policy will be to 'de-stream'. The methods and inevitable consequences of such a further scheme are set out in the later issues of the well known Educational Black Papers.

The candour of these studies is such that some regular reviewers of publications on educational theory have confessed that they are quite unable to bring themselves to read them. It appears that those concerned about basic freedoms have to contend not only with the closed shop but with the closed mind. The full measure of the destruction wrought for the next two generations was mirrored in Mrs Williams, the 1977 Secretary of State's reflection about the necessity of now erecting special centres of excellence in education. These used to be called grammar schools or direct grant schools.

In surveying the malaise caused by penal levels of taxation, the ill health of the National Health Scheme and the tragic politicalizing of the country's schools, two lowest common denominators emerge. Firstly, freedom of choice has been the last rather than the first concern of almost every leading politician of both ruling parties in the whole now long post-war period. Secondly, no post-war government has stopped to ask itself the simple question—what is the purpose of government? In answering this question we reach the nub of freedom. Are executive governments and their party legislatures any longer the best instrument for enabling people to better their lot and fulfil their legitimate aspirations? Or are they merely instruments for the most detailed manipulation and interference in the lives of those whose taxes sustain them? More briefly, is Government a means to an end or has it become an end in itself? The answer depends not purely on whether you are a governor and whether you are one of the governed. It depends whether or not, like that greatest of freedom fighters John Lilburne (1614–57), you believe that freedom is a birthright. The plea for freedom is an appeal *beyond* a parliamentary system which has become an elective dictatorship. Freedom has a unique authority vested in the ultimate sovereignty of the people themselves.

Lady Morrison of Lambeth

Freedom and the Family

> That is the secret of happiness and virtue, liking what you have got to do. All conditions aim at that—making people like their unescapable social destiny.
>
> ALDOUS HUXLEY

The family structure of man, woman and their children is biologically inherent in man's nature. Indeed, without it he would not have evolved, could not have evolved and would certainly never have become the first among the creatures of the earth. It rests on the length of time taken by a human being to mature or, more basically, the length of time during which a child is entirely dependent on adults for its sustenance, its safety, its very life and during which the child would certainly perish without devoted if not loving attention. To protect such an organization as the family, nature has implanted strong maternal and paternal instincts, so deeply rooted and so strong, that only fools, or worse, could attempt to deny their existence or seek to eradicate them.

Studies have been made in many countries on abandoned or motherless children, orphaned through tyranny or natural disaster, who have been brought up in institutions or concentration camps. All studies of such children, even those reared by enlightened minders in model institutions, reveal the evidence of impoverished personalities as a result of lack of close human relationships. For raising children is a sacrificial but vital profession; time-consuming and uneconomic in a direct sense.

For example, if it is argued that the safety and sustenance of the child over many years can very well be provided by other adults and not necessarily by the parents, it must be admitted.

that this is so. But such dedicated attention will still only be given by those with the equally deeply implanted instincts of maternal or paternal love. And where will these attributes be more efficiently used than in the care of one's own children? No one will deny the love and care that many are capable of giving the offspring of others; the fact remains they are but substitute parents: the children but substitutes for their own.

So that to pretend that 'the family' is an invention of man designed solely to bind man to some form or other of economic organization is surely one of the ugliest lies of our time. It takes what is best and deepest in man, cheapens it, smears it and mocks at it. And at the same time the very basis of the family is under attack by campaigns for women's 'liberation'; by demands for the State to foster and nourish, to take greater and greater responsibility for the well-being of the child, inevitably, finally to be solely responsible. This is the greatest challenge to freedom because it sets the State and institutions above the human being.

Even in Britain today, as more and more freedoms are encroached upon, it seems unthinkable that the State would wish to undermine the family. Yet in the Soviet Union, in 1917, the Bolsheviks' 'future paradise' was envisaged without the impediment of family loyalties. They attacked the whole concept by insisting that each child was a small property of the State and a responsibility of the community. After the general breakdown of law and order, misery and demoralization, they had to reinstate the family once more, having discovered disastrously that an institution without families could not exist. But imagine the far-reaching results of the following story in undermining family loyalties and ties. It was held up as a shining example to all Russian school children between eight and twelve years of age, as an obligatory set-book parable in the early years of Stalin's reign up to 1939.

Pavlik Morosov was the eleven-year-old son of a landowning peasant, or kulak, who plotted against collectivization in the Soviet Union in 1931. Eavesdropping on a meeting which took place in their house one evening between his father and collaborators, Pavlik reported his father's clandestine plan to the Secret Police, the NKVD (now the KGB) and the father, on discovering his son's disloyalty, killed the boy.

Pavlik Morosov became a textbook hero of Russia's youth for betraying his own father. Conversely, today, in the Soviet Union, you can get a court order to force your own child or sibling to support you with maintenance payments, thereby relieving the State of welfare responsibility. (What a far cry from British law in which a wife cannot be forced to testify against her husband, however criminal.)

If we feel secure in comparison to such a state of affairs, let us not be complacent. Freedom, like air, is everywhere about us, unnoticed, uncherished and only fervently desired when we stand to lose it. Only those of us with bitter experience or clear vision can see its erosion and the shadow of inevitable tyranny approaching; yet few of those are in a position to convey to the unvigilant or apathetic their own sense of foreboding, let alone convince them.

In the pursuit of happiness the element of freedom has many facets. Those among us who embrace ideologies alien to our history and age-long habits tend to forget or deceitfully overlook in their propaganda all the points which the democratic powers fought for so persistently for inclusion in what is known as 'Basket III' of the Helsinki Accord and which is closely linked with family life. This includes re-unification of families split by the man-made barrier referred to as the Iron Curtain. The very same contraption is an obstacle of free travel. It is well-nigh impossible for a Pole, Czech or Romanian to travel as an individual to the Soviet Union and it is certainly not only the shortage of hard currencies in all the Soviet bloc countries which limits the number of people who can visit the West. And to be more specific, for a whole family to undertake such a trip is almost unthinkable. The wife or child has to stay behind as a hostage. This is also true of diplomats.

Western women's magazines, ideal-home reviews and similar 'bourgeois' literature are frowned upon in East-Central Europe by the local authorities and publications of this type when sent as gifts seldom reach their destination.

To revert to a purely family affair: for a Westerner on a mission or on holiday in the countries of the Communist-controlled hemisphere to fall in love with a local girl is the beginning of a thorny path to happiness which is from time to time well illustrated in our press and which occupies a lot of the time of the Foreign Offices of the democratic alliance.

All this should be kept in mind by those who seek to destroy our freedoms instead of improving them or merely arresting their decline.

In considering the freedom affecting us today it is quite apparent that there is an insidious decline in most standards affecting the family. It is reflected in many fields and as a child is reared and develops, it is subjected to pressures in the home due to the economic climate, through the Welfare State, in school, college and finally, as an adolescent, by certain of the mass media, law and authority.

When dealing with the subject 'Freedom and the Family' and whatever conclusions we arrive at—we can always look back to the 'Book of books', the Bible and there we find in a precise though simple form the norm or rule which in the end should be unalterable because it is both sensible and practicable. I am thinking for instance of what is the Biblical concept of family relationship which one can find in Colossians:

Wives, submit yourselves unto your own husbands, as it is fit in the Lord. —Husbands, love your wives and be not bitter against them. —Children, obey your parents in all things: for this is well pleasing unto the Lord. (3, 18–20)

Elementary, one might comment, but if religious instruction were to be eliminated from our educational system, have we a better 'textbook' for children for the fundamental laws of decent and purposeful life? Perhaps later on other quotations will illustrate the kind of guidance which ought to be considered even in complicated situations.

In 1946 when reunited families looked forward to rebuilding their old life together, it seemed that with the British bulldog tenacity, and with incentive, they had everything to gain. But after thirty years many are now asking themselves, 'What fundamental improvements, if any, have been made in our quality of life or in our pursuit of happiness?' For example, how does their living accommodation compare with those post-war years, where the advantages of more light and privacy in some cases, has been balanced by the disadvantages of tower blocks and overcrowded homes?

As that great historian of liberty, Lord Acton wrote, 'A people averse to the institution of private property is without the first elements of freedom.' It is important then to remember that only 52% of houses in Britain are owner-occupied or are in the process of being acquired under mortgage. This most important freedom to strive to provide the roof under which he raises his family, is central to a father's sense of purpose and achievement.

According to one report, and to the National Society for the Prevention of Cruelty to Children, the physical and social restrictions of living in high-rise flats cause serious strain to parents and their children. Councils have suspended letting such accommodation to families with children under fifteen and this problem underlines once again the dangers of adopting unproved innovations for the sake of temporary expediencies.

The worst thing that happened to British housing was to make the local authority the monopoly instrument for providing houses for the ordinary man. In this they have lamentably failed by providing dreary housing, instantly recognizable as such, whereas the speculative builder has offered economy and style and has endeavoured to satisfy the desires of his customers by making such basics as kitchens and bathrooms both functional and attractive. This may be done with self-interest but, as Milton Friedman observes, this is not a corrupt but a sensible and social dynamic.

Above all, the pride of ownership, without interference from anybody, is a basic need for most of us and the salutary effects of it are obvious for all to see where there are streets of identical houses owned by the local authority and by private owners, due to the legalizing of the sale of municipally owned property. In the first case there is an air of lack of interest and neglect and in the second, one of tidiness and care. Many small skills must be passed on in these homes at mother's or father's elbow, with broom or screwdriver, and the first seeds of practical education and application are sown.

In the case of a declining industry, such as the cotton industry in Lancashire after 1910, an owner looking for other employment was able to sell and move to another area instead of being tied down to the inevitable restrictions of finding work in the immediate vicinity, with all the attendant frustrations to his wife and children. Also the privately rented sector in housing, progressively throttled by more and more Rent Restriction legislation since 1918, continues to decline and there is developing a local authority monopoly in rented accommodation, so that families who wish to rent a home are restricted to little or no choice.

The left-wingers have wanted fundamentally to keep their clutches on control of local authority housing because it has an immense but sometimes imagined electoral importance.

The whittling down of freedom of choice in education is another facet of a threat to our society through the family. It is the first principle of good government that it shall maximize the choice open to its masters, the governed, within ecologically definable limits. This ideal has been continually violated. A further serious reduction in choice was brought about by the Butler Education Act in 1944. While this Act at least acknowledged the realistic need for education according to age, aptitude and ability, the basic flaw was that the State was looked upon as a virtual monopoly supplier of education. The system predictably became more and more dependent on the elimination of competition (by way of private education and that provided by religious foundations), and more and more hostile to selection on the grounds that this was divisive.

This trend of course leads to another aspect of the devaluation of freedoms, for it limits the citizen's choice in spending his honestly earned and taxed income.

The dictates of genetics, of evolution and of developmental biology all demonstrate that individuals vary both in rates and sequences of development. Children are in fact gloriously unequal. Just when the bureaucrats and millenarian educationalists inform us that they have everything cut and dried, human nature puts the cat amongst the pigeons. Educating our children according to a single newfangled concept which ignores the evolutionary time-scale, diversity and selection, is positively asking for a steep decline in civilized standards. It is a supreme irony that today, in the Soviet Union, there is more and more of a trend towards elitist education whilst we have passed the disastrous Comprehensive Bill thus coercing parents to send their children to schools some of which are so unsuccessful they have not gained a single 'O' or 'A' level in an entire academic year.

In 1965 in *Education and the State*, Dr E. G. West gave evidence that literacy and numeracy were widespread and spreading by 1870. Dr West concluded that the State was therefore jumping on a 'galloping horse' when it made education compulsory the following year. In 1975 he gave evidence that the percentage rates were tailing off.

Apart from the controversies over curricula, streaming, mixed abilities, examination, selection and class sizes, there are more sinister developments threatening the freedom of our students. At the inaugural meeting of the Revolutionary Socialist Students' Federation, 1,000 students from Leeds, Manchester, Hull, Essex, Sussex, Oxford, Cambridge and the London School of Economics combined to launch a plan in March 1969 to establish 'Red Bases' in universities, colleges and technical institutions. The casual reader of a report on this attendance, would most probably put the attendance down to youthful assertiveness but there is no doubt that with their energy and determination these students are well suited to infiltrate all teaching establishments in order to provide springboards for their revolutionary campaigns. They stated, 'We are more concerned with revolution in capitalist society as a whole than in mere student power.' As Charles Péguy put it, so simply, 'Tyranny is always better organised than freedom,' and like all revolutionary groups, this Federation aims to destroy, not improve, our existing way of life. How far removed all this is from the classic and human purpose of education—that is, to maximize potential.

Just as it is evident that the public educational system in Britain is threatened with breakdown, so it is that the smog of inflation and economic instability weaves its way through family life and is the most potent threat to its freedom, choking its well-being.

Lord Rothschild said that 'if Britain's disappointing rate of economic growth persisted, then by the 1980s the people of Britain would become the peasants of Europe.' Whilst the present trend seems benign and gentle, engineering the Welfare State, 'free' education, 'free' medicine and a kaleidoscope of subsidies it is in fact destructive to the responsibility of self respect and dignity of human beings as their incentive to work is crushed and they observe others gaining more from unemployment plus a little 'on the side'. Present-day bureaucracy is the business of ever more detailed interference in the lives of its subjects. As Ludwig von Mises, the Austrian economist, wrote, 'They promise the blessings of the Garden of Eden but plan to transform the world into a gigantic post office'. In addition, the family economic stability is unsettled by such pressures on the bread-winner as the closed shop, industrial disputes and VAT.

Young people need intelligent, steady discipline in the home and school, and upon this teaching their mental, physical and moral welfare depend. Firstly they need standards in unselfishness and diligence, loyalty, marriage and family life. Marriage is an institution and the home life which grows from marriage, is seriously threatened by incest, promiscuity, adultery, child molestation, prostitution and homosexual practices, all of which are deviant patterns which distort and demean human sexuality.

The New Testament in Hebrews wastes no words on what is moral or immoral. Chapter 13, verse 4 makes the 'law':

Marriage is honourable in all, and the bed undefiled; but whoremongers and adulterers God will judge.

It was John Stuart Mill who believed that freedom was intended for adults only: it was inappropriate that children should have liberty. Thus it became the duty of parents to train children in readiness to exercise freedom for themselves. In the past, freedom did not enter into a child's upbringing for it was the parents who made the laws in the home: the laws which were passed on from one generation to another.

In modern times, however, the authority of parents is being eroded by harmful literature, television programmes and certain teachers who fail to recognize the value of self-discipline.

Although there has always been a tendency for creative and intelligent children to react against the despotic attitude of parents it is mainly in recent years that the younger generation have reacted so violently against their parents' standards.

There are those who believe it would be hard to measure the degree of damage caused to the young in the late sixties by some pop stars' example of promiscuity and drug-taking. But a further danger for present-day families is the increasingly materialistic atmosphere of a society which aims to capture the teenage market with offers of bigger and better goods to be paid for later; temptations for young mothers to return to work thereby neglecting their small children, and entertainment in the form of plays, novels, etc. which depict the dishonest and immoral as being acceptable.

These and other factors combine to erode the influence formerly exercised by parents and it is noticed that those children who stray from the formerly approved guidelines find themselves lost and unhappy.

The immediate post-war years were not influenced at all by television which has, during the last thirty years, dominated the mass media. It is true that there are some programmes of excellence for children or adults, educative and stimulating, but materialism in advertising and films is constantly thrust at the viewer along with sick pop artists represented as gods to delirious teenagers. Standards of censorship slip lower and lower, X-films and pornography are at the disposal of any teenager determined to pursue them and anything not penalized soon becomes 'acceptable'.

Lord Denning has called this material 'propaganda for promiscuity and perversion', and there is no doubt that the more laws are relaxed, the more the young will be exploited by sex perversion and by those handling pornographic literature or merchandise for their own huge financial gain.

The Council of Civil Liberties supports the lowering of the age of consent to fifteen or even fourteen. If this were the case the fact would be included in sex-education in schools and mentioned on every television line in the country, resulting in more child promiscuity without a doubt.

The largest band of militant homosexuals in this country includes special groups for students and is making determined efforts to enter schools with propaganda for homosexuality. While dangerous situations like this prevail the young are desperately in need of the help of authority and laws to protect them.

It is encouraging that on all sides, from people in the media, in the Church, from politicians and educationalists, we hear outcries against permissiveness, degenerating standards and destructive policies. Yet the Home Office and its advisers demonstrably lack the will to coax the country back to higher moral levels. Unfortunately religion is often ignored and seems to be in a state of change itself with regard to abortion and euthanasia, thus confusing its followers. And so they might turn to the State for guidance but where it is lacking it is unlikely that they will have much to emulate in the contemporary moral climate.

It is even possible that freedom of speech, still so strongly upheld in this country, is not as helpful to freedom's cause as it might seem, in that it acts as a palliative to that percentage of our population who are writers or broadcasters able to express their views. They are thus neutralized from being a more potent catalyst. But the ordinary man, unaware of the writings of intellectuals or cynical of the differing political views showered upon him, will know nothing about the gathering storm until he is at least uncomfortable, by which time it will be too late to stem the tide. Not that we should dream of anything other than freedom of speech, but a giant problem still remains as to how to get through to those who think so little (and read even less) about the consequences of a 'soft' or demoralized society.

Solzhenitsyn warns:

Westerners will need a great deal of strength, of resolution, to see and accept the evidence of the implacable tide of violence and bloodshed that has methodically, steadily, triumphantly radiated out from a single centre for nearly sixty years, and to locate the countries already lined up for the next holocaust.

Yet still the families gallop on towards the cliff edge, bent on their superficial standard of living, pursuing *la dolce vita*. Even the most basic constituents of everyday life of a poor family in Britain would seem luxurious beside those of families in countries where they are no longer free. Will we not heed such men of conscience as Solzhenitsyn, Sakharov and Bukovsky who so courageously defend victims of the Soviet regime, suffering under psychiatric 'treatment', torture from prolonged hunger, solitary confinement, bitter cold and hard labour? Or will we prefer the temporary fools' paradise of our own peace and quiet to their liberty?

Where is the leader who can save the nation, as Churchill did in the last world war? Where is he who will not budge a centimetre in the face of tyranny and who will lead the country in setting exemplary moral standards? In 1940 when Churchill sat with his Cabinet in committee and the reports were of defeat from every side, someone asked desperately, 'What *can* we do?'

'Do? Do?' exclaimed Churchill preposterously, 'Why, fight of course! And hang from the nearest lamp-post! You can choose yours. I'll have the one at the end of the street.'

We must never take freedom for granted. For the sake of the family, which surely embraces every man, woman and child on earth, we must cherish it and fight for it; for our lives.

Russell Lewis

Freedom of Speech and Publication

It is heartening that at the time of writing* there is one example—I refer to India—of a country where attempts to stifle freedom of speech have been magnificently reversed. Yet this, sad to say, is not the general pattern in the world as we see it today, where freedom by and large is in retreat. Broadly speaking there is the growing Socialist bloc where freedom of speech and expression is greatly curtailed; there is the third world where the picture is mixed but usually the tune is called by dictatorships, where whatever freedoms are enjoyed are at the mercy of the dictator's whim. Finally there is the Western world where, at first glance, freedom of expression has never been more unqualified and unrestrained.

Certainly this is true as regards content, for there was never a time which was more permissive and when 'anything went'. Yet this impression is rather misleading because, while the limitations placed upon freedom of expression by State authority have been diminishing, the restraints placed upon writers, editors and publishers by other bodies, notably trade unions, students and other protest organizations, have been growing in the most insidious way. This is all the worse when such bodies are actively engaged in subverting the very freedoms from which they themselves gain.

It is therefore time to take stock of the freedom which we enjoy in the West and to consider just exactly what are the conditions

* March 1977

of that enjoyment. For the current prescription, to which most people pay lip-service, is that that liberty should be absolute, that any denial even in order to protect the greater part of it, is unacceptable to any liberal-minded person, and that the choice is really between freedom unlimited and totalitarianism.

If this statement seems to be exaggerated consider the following assertion in a book about the National Council of Civil Liberties, entitled *Civil Liberties in Britain*.[1]

Freedom is to be able to gather together in a room above the public bar to promote a revolution. It is for several thousand people preaching that revolution to be able to march through a city without being shot at, beaten up or arrested without cause. It is for passport holding citizens to be able to come and go at will. It is for magazine editors to be able to publish foul-mouthed political nonsense without risk of fine or imprisonment.

It would be a mistake to think that this is a cranky example, unrepresentative of what is intellectually respectable. On the contrary what is considered to be the classic exposition of the liberal Western position about freedom of speech, namely John Stuart Mill's essay *On Liberty*, states[2] '. . . there ought to exist the fullest liberty of professing and discussing, as a matter of ethical conviction, any doctrine, however immoral it might be considered.' This is the time-honoured description of what has now come to be called the open society, and any society which does not allow such unbridled freedom is considered to fall short of the liberal ideal and in fact to be closed.

Does this matter, or is it just of academic interest? Well, it is important because this is the usual argument in terms of which our noble concept of freedom of expression is defended. It is in my belief a dangerous form of justification because it brings to the forefront rather unnecessarily the paradox of freedom—that unless we ensure to the enemies of freedom the liberties which they are keen to abuse, then we deny the essence of what we ultimately stand for and are in consequence no better than those to whom we are opposed.

Admittedly there is nothing new about this dilemma. It was, I think, Father Ronald Knox who made the debating point (at a time when the Catholic Church had more exclusive claims than it has now) that he could claim the right to silence his opponents because that was his principle while also claiming the right to be heard by liberal democrats because that was their principle. The difference from his day is that those who are the current foes of freedom are a great deal more formidable than the Catholic Church even in the days of the Inquisition. The views of Voltaire, who knew the Catholic Church when it was at its persecuting worst, have been condensed as, 'I disapprove of what you say, but I will defend to the death your right to say it.' Yet that high-minded sentiment looks pretty sick if the one professing it immediately goes down in a hail of machine-gun bullets.

Let us then look at the Millite, essentially pacifist, view of freedom of speech a little more closely, for so far we have only taken its conclusion. Why is it necessary to have the fullest possible liberty of speech? Because, says Mill, that is the only way to ensure that truth will prevail. If an opinion is true then in open competition with false opinions it is bound to win through, and then truth will not only out but is the more fully vindicated by the exposure of error. Besides in complicated matters where the opinions being put forward are partly true and partly false the true elements in each case will show through.[3] And of course Mill and his disciples feel that it is hardly worth spending much time in proving that a society organized in the light of truth must be the best, and most progressive sort.

Now it seems to me that accepting the Millite idea of society as a truth-seeking affair would not necessarily be difficult for a Marxist. For if we, like Jesting Pilate, ask, 'What is truth?' then presumably we must answer 'correspondence with reality'. And what is reality? 'Why,' says the Marxist, 'it is the world process which is made manifest through Marx's dialectic.' 'How do you know that?' we may well ask, and back would come the reply, 'on the authority of Marx', or better still, 'by study of the dialectic itself which absorbs the kind of discussion through which Mill believed truth to be established.' In the end the Millite would have to argue the toss with the Marxist about the basis of knowledge, and say that it consists mainly of sense-data and logical propositions, while the Marxist would say that both these were subsumed in the dialectic—which is about as far as one can go.

On this philosophical argument the Millites I think have the edge on the Marxists whose position is exposed as being basically authoritarian and resting as much as any religion (which of course it is) on revelation.

The weaker side of the Millite argument is that, as an American scholar Willmoore Kendall has pointed out,[4] it rests on a false premise about the nature of society:

They assume that society is, so to speak, a debating club, devoted above all to the pursuit of truth, and capable therefore of subordinating itself—and all other considerations, goods, and goals, to that pursuit.

Yet we know full well that society is not in fact a debating club, and that if it were—like the General Assembly of the United Nations for example—'the chances of its adopting the pursuit of truth are negligible.' It is more realistic to assume that societies value all sorts of objectives including most notably their own survival, or the enjoyment of life, individual and collective, which its citizens have. It may therefore be wise and proper to suppress and keep suppressed certain information—like the activities of the country's intelligence services for example—instead of revealing the whole truth about them. Priority for the pursuit of truth is indeed a minority interest. That does not make it unimportant. Indeed the more sensible argument should be to say that allowing the minority which is so addicted to go its own way is wise and sensible in the general interest. That is very different from saying that all questions in society are open questions. Indeed perhaps the best example of a society so far which was like that was probably Weimar Germany—and look what happened to that!

Yet even in a debating society there have to be general rules, for instance on how the debate may be conducted. Or again, if one talks of free competition in ideas on the analogy of the marketplace, one should remember that the existence of a market presupposes rules of behaviour, protection against fraud, the enforcement of contracts, etc. This is only to say that freedom of speech and publication, on which so much attention is concentrated in the West, cannot be really separated from other kinds of freedom, that indeed the degree and kind of freedom of speech in a community at any one time will reflect the structure of power in that community. Restraints on freedom will generally reflect the values of the socially dominant group. On the same line of reasoning the best chance for freedom of speech as of any kind of freedom is a balance, and preferably also a diffusion of social power among different groups. That is to say that a pluralist society is the best guarantee of freedom or, if not guarantee, at least the general condition in which freedom is most likely to survive and prosper, given that the people concerned have also the desire for freedom.

This may look like a rather mechanistic view, but it can be sustained and given life by reference to a few of the more prominent historical examples.

The usual starting point for any historical disquisition on freedom and especially free speech is ancient Athens. The Athenians had the wisdom at an early stage to appoint a remarkable man called Solon to give them a constitution. He retained for the upper classes the right of making and administering laws and put on them the whole burden of taxes. The poor were exempt from direct taxes but were excluded from office, but he allowed them to elect magistrates. Power was commensurate with public service. That is how the poor who manned the ships which contributed to the defeat of the Persians, were given the opportunity of office. Yet Pericles, under whom Greek democracy came to its apogee, restricted the right of citizenship to the Athenians of pure descent, so that the poor citizens became roughly equal in number to the patricians. It was when this delicate balance was destroyed that freedom gave way to the tyranny of the majority, and, as Lord Acton the great Liberal Catholic historian at the turn of the century put it in one of his essays, 'They plundered the rich until they conspired with the public enemy, and they crowned their guilt by the martyrdom of Socrates.'

The trouble with the Athenians was their volatility, or, to put it another way, their 'all questions are open questions' society. For they probably came nearer than any people in history to Mill's ideal of treating all opinions as equal, indeed to enthroning scepticism, and very corrosive the result was. They were the classic negative proof of Bagehot's point that stupidity is a great political virtue, stupidity in the sense of lack of a critical attitude towards institutions. For it is more important to work and enjoy the institutions than for ever to be analysing them. It was in this that lay the superior practical wisdom of the ancient Romans. At this distance we tend to think of the great age of the Antonines as being one of benign dictatorship. Yet this is to miss the point that the Roman Empire was much more in the nature of a federation of free cities. It was when this federation flourished that Rome had its great age of literature and saw the greatest extension of freedom under the law with the rights of Roman citizens shared with the people of the provinces. It was only later, in the time of Diocletian, when the burdens of taxation to pay for a large army and a gross bureaucracy had reduced the cities to bankruptcy, that their free civic life disappeared and a network of tax spies spread across the whole of the Empire.

In retrospect a remarkable feature of the whole of the ancient world was that there was no distinction understood between Church and State. That is why the Caesars were not only emperors but gods. Loyalty to the State also meant a pinch of incense offered before the Emperor's statue. It took centuries to work out this distinction through the experience of the conflict in Western Europe between Church and State, between Empire and Papacy, and that distinction is an element in our liberty today. To us religious unbelief is not the same thing as being a traitor. The Russians did not share this experience which belonged to the territories of the Church of Rome in the West of Europe. They inherited the concept of the Byzantine Church which was firmly under the thumb of the secular ruler. The Russians should be understood as still continuing that tradition because Communism is in reality a religion—a State religion—and loyalty to Communism is regarded as identical with loyalty to the Soviet State.

Before arriving at the present accepted Western concept of a division of the temporal and the spiritual, our ancestors had to go through a period of theocracy, of ecclesiastical imperialism (when both religious and secular power were concentrated in Rome). It was no mere coincidence that the age of faith was also an age of persecution.

It is a paradox that the coming of the Renaissance, meant to be freeing of the Western mind from feudal bonds, also brought a greater measure of persecution. Yet we should remember that the Renaissance State was much more concentrated and efficient than the Medieval State and it was this concentration of power which made persecution more effective.

Religious toleration came ultimately from the break-up of the unity of the Western Church. In England the multiplication of sects led to considerable toleration of different religious belief under Cromwell, and with this freedom of religious opinion came the plea for a wider freedom of publication. Milton in his *Areopagitica* (1644) made a most eloquent and moving case for the liberty of unlicensed printing. As he said, if the waters of truth 'flow not in a perpetual progression they sicken into a muddy pool of conformity and tradition.' Perhaps it is because of Milton that we tend to place the freedom of thought above civil liberty. As he said, 'Give me the liberty to know, to utter and to argue freely according to conscience above all other liberties.'

It was with the revolutionary settlement that religious toleration became the general rule in Britain, though the variety of different sects emigrating to America in search of religious liberty had already led to toleration becoming the norm on the other side of the Atlantic. The doctrine of religious tolerance also found expression in the famous 'Letter' on the subject by the distinguished philosopher of the Revolution, John Locke, in 1689. He said that since true religion consists 'in the inward and full persuasion of the mind', and the magistrate's power 'consists only in outward force', then it is absurd for the State to make laws to enforce religion. The interesting thing is the exceptions he allowed from this sweeping argument. For, although he was prepared to give full toleration to heathens like the Indians of North America, he would not tolerate Roman Catholics because they 'teach that faith is not to be kept with heretics', that 'kings excommunicated forfeit their crowns and kingdoms,' and because they deliver themselves up to the protection and service of a foreign prince—the Pope. Clearly Locke saw the Catholics of his day in much the same light as many see the Communists today, as politically unreliable, indeed potential traitors. He made a further exception in the case of atheists, because 'Those are not all to be tolerated who deny the being of God. Promises, covenants and oaths, which are the bonds of human society, can have no hold upon an atheist.'

It seems to me that later liberal writers like J. B. Bury who treated these exceptions as the aberrations of a great mind limited by his time[5] did not fully appreciate the danger of religious subversives who were a real threat in the time of Locke to the security of the State. After all the Jacobites made two attempts to overthrow the régime in the next half century.

There remained after the Glorious Revolution of 1688 a number of disabilities laid upon the Nonconformists and Catholics which it took a considerable time to lift, such as the Test Acts which kept them out of the old universities, which were not removed until 1870. Yet Britain was still an example to most of Continental Europe. In France Voltaire waged a great campaign against the continuing persecution by the French Church. Voltaire was a deist and his was the religion of reason. One might have thought that the French Revolution, when it came, would have meant immediate toleration of all religious opinions. Yet, as had happened in history all too painfully often, those who had been the persecuted became the persecutors. Robespierre like Voltaire was a deist and he celebrated the feast of reason with a celebration during which a tart danced on the altar of Notre Dame. France was formally dechristianized and the worship of the Supreme Being propagated. The creed of Liberty, Equality and Fraternity was the creed of the new religion, and terror was used to bring the heretics to heel, just as terror is used against the Baptists and other Christians and the Jews and Moslems in present-day Russia: these are the modern heretics who will not worship dialectical materialism.

In the course of the nineteenth century toleration spread over the continent, and freedom of opinion which had usually been regulated by the Church became more widespread. No one at the turn of this century could have imagined to what an extent the trend towards freedom of thought and expression would have been reversed and new fanaticisms, in effect new state religions—Nazism, Communism, Maoism, more all-embracing, more demanding in the loyalty they expected from their supporters, more terrifying in their techniques (of brainwashing etc.) and more ruthless in dealing with dissidents than any other faiths in history—were to be let loose on mankind.

As is well known, in present-day Russia, those who attempt to practise their faith in Christianity or any other religion, especially if they are young, are consistently harassed and often imprisoned or put into what are euphemistically called 'mental asylums' where they are given drugs which cause them pain, actually make them insane, or damage their mental faculties, for instance making them unable to concentrate, so that many would prefer an ordinary prison camp. Others have been deprived of their children who are forcibly taken away to be educated and brought up as atheists. Besides these overt forms of persecution there are indirect pressures like depriving dissidents of their ration books or preventing them from having a job.

Of course it is not only religious dissidents or human rights campaigners who suffer. Those who do not agree with the official line on any academic subject are likely to land in difficulties. The most notorious case was that of Professor Michurin who was hounded to his death for not agreeing with the official line on biology, which had been laid down by the egregious Lysenko[6] that acquired characteristics can be inherited—a long exploded theory of Lamarck. This was almost in the same class as Hitler's insistence that scientists must accept that Aryan atoms are different from the atoms of other races.

This kind of unfreedom in ideas and their expression is clearly related to the fact that the ruling party bureaucratic élite in Moscow is a small, highly privileged group with a tight grip on power. Indeed there has probably never been in history such a highly organized system for protecting the interest of the ruling group where non-compliance can often quite literally mean starvation. What better example of the dangers of concentration of power particularly the uniting of economic and political power in the same hands!

The dangers of Socialism bringing tyranny have often been pointed out. Yet, in the British context, the idea has never been taken very seriously. When Mr Churchill took literally that brilliant tract of Professor Hayek, *The Road to Serfdom*, and made a speech during the 1945 General Election about how Socialism would lead to the establishment of a gestapo in Britain, it was generally considered to be one of the greatest blunders of his career. Nobody could believe that dear old Clem Attlee could ever become a dictator, and of course any such idea would have been repugnant to that worthy man. Yet, in the fullness of time, we have come in Britain to the point where the threat of suppression of freedom of expression is a palpable one, not through the setting up of a censorship but through the mining and sapping of the present pluralist ownership and control of the institutions through which that freedom is expressed, and even, what we now come to, their total absorption.

This threat was spelt out in the report of a Labour Party study group chaired by Mr Anthony Wedgwood Benn in July 1974, a report called *The People and the Media*. The significance of Benn's chairmanship was that he had already made himself prominent for his extreme views of the idea of industrial participation especially in the media. Indeed he told the Labour Party conference in October 1972:

I sometimes wish the trades unionists who work in the mass media— those who are writers, broadcasters, secretaries, printers and lift operators in Thomson House—would remember that they too are members of our working class movement and have a responsibility to see that what is said about us is true.

In this report therefore it was perhaps predictable that the press was to be put under a Communications Council. The crucial point, however, related to advertising revenue, because, while advertisers were to retain their right to choose which publications to advertise in, the fees would be collected and distributed by a new Advertising Revenue Board. Papers successful in attracting advertisements would see their earnings redistributed among their weaker brethren. There seemed to be no suspicion among the authors of the report that the advertising revenue is not unlimited and its flow not invulnerable to their antics.

Another piece of perverted ingenuity related to newsprint, under which preferential prices were to be offered to 'minority publications' (*Labour Weekly*, *Militant* or *Red Dwarf?*). The cost of subsidizing this cheap newsprint again was to come from the pool of advertising revenue.

Not content with that, the cost of trying to launch and establish a new newspaper would also be subsidized from the same abundant source.

And of course there was to be worker participation in industry.

Nor was that all, because the report also covered broadcasting. It proposed the dismantling of both the BBC and the Independent Broadcasting Authority and the transfer of their powers to a powerful Broadcasting Commission. On the same lines as the recommendations for the press, the advertising revenue was to be milked, with the taxpayer chipping in where necessary to top up the revenue. There was also to be a Communications Council to keep a watching brief on all mass media and to act as a sort of Star Chamber where people could come and make complaints.

Commercial radio was to be scrapped. Programme makers were to have no revenue of their own—once licence fees had been abolished—and everyone would be obliged to go cap in hand to the Public Broadcasting Commission. Admittedly no one is at present seriously proposing to put any of this into immediate effect, but experience suggests that in contemporary Britain the extremism of today becomes the orthodoxy of tomorrow.

One thing is clear—that there would be little freedom of the press or broadcasting under this programme. And to say this is not to impugn the intentions of Mr Benn, who very likely thinks that these arrangements would make for more liberty of expression. It is simply that if all this power were concentrated in one body, sooner or later it would be riding roughshod over all opinions other than those of the ruling clique. For, as Adam Smith said long ago, 'It is not from the benevolence of the butcher, the brewer or the baker that we expect our dinners but from regard to their own interest',[7] which through an 'invisible hand' promotes the general interest. In the Benn set-up there would be a reversal of this process so that through the invisible hand of the bureaucracy and the political establishment, the benevolence of those in charge would direct the production of what the consumer did not want including the denial of information and views that he wanted to hear, or wanted to express. The institutions are more often most valuable in the results they produce despite the motives of those who work them, and it is the prime and never finished task of the good society to provide or improve the institutions of government so that they can be operated without particular damage to the ruled by rulers who are neither very capable nor especially good.

At present the danger to freedom of expression does not come so much from this source as from the unions acting on their own account, especially with the aid of new legislation which Labour has been trying to put through.

Before we look at the legislation it is worth considering an example of what was happening even before the Labour Government took power.

Thus, during the February 1974 election campaign, Aims of Industry, a body supporting free enterprise, was conducting two advertising campaigns—one against Labour's nationalization policies and the other against the extremists in the trade unions. They succeeded in advertising in the *Guardian, The Times, Daily Mail, New Statesman* and *Spectator*, and some provincial newspapers. In some cases the print unions insisted, as a condition of their appearing, that their own advertisement should appear alongside. Many newspapers, however, banned these adverts altogether. Aims of Industry was told by many journalists that, though they found the news of this banning very interesting, they doubted whether their story would be published. Again they were told by those in charge of radio and television programmes that they could not use stories about the role of the extreme left, or that these were objectionable because they would produce 'imbalance'.

A more serious case developed when Lord Astor was prevented from making comment on press freedom in his own newspaper, the *Observer*, because of the action of the printers' union, who, by their action of course underlined the very warning which he was seeking to put across to the public.

The 'Press Freedom' issue really came to the forefront with the attempt by Mr Michael Foot, when Secretary for Employment to give trade unions the right to organize closed shops—a right which had been restricted by the Conservative Industrial Relations Act of 1971. Under the Foot Bill a person who refused to join a particular union specified in a membership agreement between a union and an employer could be dismissed without any statutory redress. As this Bill coincided with a growth in activity and militancy among the National Union of Journalists it was feared that the NUJ might manage to establish a monopoly, pushing out the less militant Institute of Journalists and be in a position to exert discipline over editors, seeking to tell them what they could publish. Or it could exclude certain journalists, of whom militants disapproved, from membership—thus depriving them of their livelihood if non-members were prevented from getting into print. When the newspaper editors protested to Mr Foot, who of course had himself been deputy editor of the *Evening Standard* and editor of the *Tribune* (and had had quite a reputation in his day as a freedom fighter e.g. when arguing against newspapers which brought actions to muzzle *Private Eye*) he showed what he was really made of by replying 'I see no difference between the free flow of information and the free flow of sewage.' The bill was defeated in the House of Lords and thereafter there has been discussion about some compromise to be enshrined in a press charter to protect editorial freedom. Since then there has been action by counter-militants (Bernard Levin and others) within the NUJ aimed at stopping the leftists. Nor has this come too soon. Yet there has also meantime been developing a new NUJ attempt to exert monopoly powers by inducing certain local authorities to refuse to deal with any journalists who do not belong to it. The motions of the left-wingers for the April 1977 NUJ delegates' meeting showed how they were hoping things would move. Some sought the support of the TUC in order to oppose the recruitment of journalists to any union other than the NUJ. In particular they wanted to put pressure for all TUC-affiliated unions to withdraw from all organizations which accord recognition to the rival Institute of Journalists. There is still in operation an NUJ rule which could at any time be put into effect which requires members not to act 'by commission or omission against the interests of the union'. This could mean that a journalist was required to forget about his prime duty of reporting and commenting on matters of public interest and weighing whether there was anything he had to say which was or was not in the interests of the National Union of Journalists.

A danger to freedom from an unexpected quarter was revealed November 1976 when a dispute hit the firm of Grunwick Processing, which processes photographs in a factory in Willesden. As 84% of the business of the firm was conducted through the post it was obviously heavily dependent on the postal system. Therefore when the Postal Workers' Union announced that it was taking 'sympathetic action' in support of the Grunwick workers by withholding deliveries of mail and refusing to accept outgoing mail from 1 November it obviously threatened the firm with bankruptcy. It was only the prompt action of the Director of the National Association for Freedom, John Gouriet, in applying for a mandatory *ex parte* injunction (on the basis that the Union of Post Office Workers was acting illegally) that saved the day.

It was not long before the day required saving again. For the Postal Workers' Union decided that it would prevent the transmission of mail and telecommunications between Britain and South Africa from midnight, 16 January, for a week, in answer to a call for action by the International Confederation of Free Trades Unions to show solidarity against the repressive attitudes towards black trade unionists in South Africa. Their way of doing so was however in breach of their statutory duty and a dangerous precedent once established. The Attorney General having failed to act, Mr Gouriet again sought and obtained an injunction from the Court of Appeal as an ordinary citizen whose rights of communication were being infringed. The post office workers backed down and the boycott was abandoned. The case was important in showing:

1   that the unions cannot break the law with impunity even for

professed idealistic purposes
2   that the Attorney General is not above the law (see pp. 6–10)
3   that the individual in a free society can always have recourse
     to the courts in defending his rights, though that recourse in
     itself presupposes the existence of independently minded in-
     dividuals with independent sources of material and financial
     support.

Yet the last point raises the big question: how long will those
independent sources survive? For there are in train changes
which could within less than a generation remove the last traces
of the independent economic activity upon which political freedoms of all kinds must in the end be based. Most obvious is the
threat of nationalization, for, as the private sector shrinks, the
sources of funds for non-Socialist activities and propaganda
must dry up. And it is not excessive to talk not only of
nationalization *tout court* but of nationalization of the national
income. In Britain Mr Roy Jenkins, while still Home Secretary,
publicly proclaimed his doubts as to whether the state spending
of over 60% of the nation's income was compatible with democracy. Besides, when so many are dependent on the government
for their employment, how many will wish to speak up in favour
of a different social order like capitalism when in the transition
to it they might find themselves out of a job? Then there are the
intermediate stages of dependence, of semi-nationalization, of
dependence on government for loans, or contracts, or planning
permission, all of which inhibit outright advocacy of a different
order of things. It will cap the lot, if the Bullock proposals for so-
called industrial democracy are ever adopted, because they have
nothing to do with industrial democracy but everything to do
with magnifying the autocracy of the union bosses. For it provides in effect for 50% representation on the company boards for
the trade union (as opposed to worker) representatives, with ap-
pointments being made by union bosses most of whom are
elected by a tiny proportion of their members. Indeed it would
give them even greater powers of patronage than are exercised by
the Prime Minister. One thing is certain: that, after it was put
through there would be no more funds from large companies for

the Conservatives, and no support for organizations like Aims of Industry or the Institute of Economic Affairs or anyone else showing any preference for the institutions of a free society.

These are examples of how the economic system is being centralized and aligned against freedom for any opinion which is contrary to the interests of the political bureaucratic élite. It is even sadder that the present student élite in the West, which will presumably be of importance in times to come, is also opposed to freedom of speech by those whom they disapprove, such as speakers whom they term right wing. There have been several incidents in recent years involving such speakers as Sir Keith Joseph and Mr Enoch Powell. The students' operative theory has been that they cannot give a platform to racists and Fascists, though obviously the true Fascists in resort to violence and suppression of rights of free speech have been themselves.

Still more disgraceful from the point of view of traditional academic freedom, Professor Hans Eysenck, when lecturing in May 1973 at the London School of Economics on race heredity and intelligence, was prevented from saying more than a few words by a Marxist–Leninist mob which invaded the lecture room and pushed him off the rostrum. His glasses were broken and his face cut by flying glass. Ironically the last time that this had happened to him had been when he had been roughed up by thugs in Germany during the Nazi era.

All of which is to say that freedom, as always, pays the price of eternal vigilance which has been exacted throughout history. Freedom of speech in particular, which we in the West at least have long taken for granted is now very far from being secure. Yet returning to this essay's point of departure, the main division of the world is between the Socialist part, where speech for the majority is very far from free, and the Western capitalist (or at least mixed economy) world where freedom of speech and expression generally, though under attack, still exists and is regarded (or so previous pages have tried to suggest) with vast complacency. This association of unfreedom with Socialism and freedom with capitalism is no matter of chance. Capitalism is, with all its faults a pluralist system, for power within it is dispersed and various, and it is this pluralism which is the necessary though not sufficient condition for freedom's existence and continuance. Socialism on the other hand does not pretend to be anything but a highly centralized system, where political and economic power are housed under the same roof and placed in the same hands. This monolithic system is the more tyrannical in the Socialist bloc because Communism, the official doctrine of the Soviet State and its satellites, is, in effect, a religion the high priests of which are the political leaders who behave like the monopoly possessors of revealed truth and who therefore proceed in the certainty that they are in the right and will be justified by history. For them any means they judge to be tactically appropriate are justified by the glorious attainment of the objective of which they alone have the true visions—as Yaroslavsky put it, 'Whatever coincides with the interests of the Proletarian Revolution is ethical.' It is the evil of monopoly of power which throughout history has proved inimical to freedom of speech or any other freedom of any consequence. It is to the principle and the institutional support of competition in ideas and beliefs that we must look for the best assurance that their consumers will be satisfied and fulfilled.

1   Barry Cox: *Civil Liberties in Britain*, Penguin 1975
2   J. S. Mill: *On Liberty*, Everyman edition p. 19, footnote
3   Ibid., Thinkers Library, 1929, pp. 63ff
4   Willmoore Kendall: 'The Open Society and its Fallacies' in *American Political Science Review*, LIV 1960, pp. 972–9
5   J. B. Bury: *History of Freedom of Thought*, Oxford University Press 1913: 'Thus Locke is not free from the prejudices of his time.' (p. 103)
6   T. D. Lysenko: 'The Situation in Biological Sciences'—*Proceedings of the Lenin Academy of Agricultural Sciences of the USSR, Session July 31–August 7, 1948*, Foreign Languages Publishing House, Moscow 1949
7   Adam Smith: *Wealth of Nations*, Everyman edition (1910), Vol. 1, p. 13

Winston S. Churchill, M.P.

Freedom and National Security

For more than thirty years the peoples of Europe—unique among the generations of the twentieth century—have enjoyed the inestimable blessings of peace. Out of the ashes and devastation of two World Wars a new Europe has been built—a Europe in which the living standard of the average family far exceeds anything dreamed of only a few years ago and which has achieved for its peoples unprecedented social and technological advance.

The peoples of Western democracies fought World War II with, above all, two goals in mind: the maintenance or restoration of their countries' freedom and the establishment of a lasting peace. There was a widespread recognition that mistakes were made in 1919 which should not be repeated in 1945, principal among these had been the oppression of the vanquished—attributed to Lloyd George in the phrase: 'We will squeeze the German lemon until the pips squeak'—and the failure to accept the right of peoples to self-determination. Thus when the United Nations was established in 1946, it was founded on the principles of self-determination and respect for human rights and had as its aim the maintenance of peace through the restraint of aggression by a world-wide system of collective security.

When the last survivors of the Nazi concentration camps were liberated, there was a general assumption in the West, whose peoples had endured, suffered and sacrificed so much, that they had won freedom, not for themselves alone, but for all mankind. Alas, it was not to be. In the moment of triumph, the wartime alliance was betrayed. The Soviet Red Army which occupied half of Europe, coming ostensibly as 'liberators' from the Nazi scourge, came in fact as a force of invasion and occupation. A generation and a half after the end of the War, more than two hundred million people of Eastern Europe continue to be denied both basic human rights as individuals and self-determination as peoples. For many, for example the Czechoslovaks, seven years of Nazi occupation has been followed by more than thirty years of Soviet occupation. In Czechoslovakia alone today there are no fewer than five Soviet divisions with more troops and tanks than Britain's entire Rhine army—they are not there as a defensive force, but as an army of occupation. In each of these countries, we see long traditions of nationhood and independence submerged under the oppressive rule of totalitarian dictatorship and the police-state.

Today a new challenge presents itself to the Western democracies and it is a challenge which, for the first time in a generation, seriously calls in question the prospects for stability in Europe and for world peace. Not content with denying human rights to their own peoples and independence to the nations of Eastern Europe, the narrow political clique wielding power in the Kremlin are in danger of disturbing the delicate equilibrium of forces which has been the foundation of world peace for more than a generation. Once again we see a single nation, ruled by a totalitarian dictatorship and motivated by an unconcealed determination to dominate the world, building up a war-machine far beyond any requirement of self-defence.

Whether the Soviet leadership has embarked on this policy of arms-escalation for the purpose of furthering aggressive military designs or to provide a strong power-base from which to wield decisive political pressure and military blackmail, is impossible to know. To argue the point is irrelevant for, whatever the intentions of the Soviet leadership today, they can change over a weekend. What is indisputable is that this build-up, together with the political designs that are behind it, represents a challenge which the Western democracies will ignore at their peril.

Our democratic society is being put to the test—at the end of the day are we to be found wanting?

The brutal challenge that confronts us inevitably, and rightly, leads us to re-examine the values on which our society is founded. Are those values still valid today? If so, are they worth defending? And, if we conclude that they are, what are we prepared to sacrifice to defend them? Are we prepared to spend as much on defence (£110.64 per head in 1976) as, for example, we spend on alcohol and tobacco (£162.46)? Are we, if need be, prepared to make the ultimate sacrifice and lay down our lives in defence of freedom, as two generations have so selflessly done before us?

What is, anyway, this thing called freedom which we in the West take so much for granted? It is not easy to define but one thing is certain, freedom is as indispensable to the life and fulfilment of the human spirit as is air to the human body. Denied freedom, the human spirit is stifled and in danger of suffocation. The old English definition of freedom as 'the power of self-determination' has the merit of treating freedom not merely as a condition of life (in which regrettably only a minority of the human race are privileged to live) but also as a state of mind for which each individual is wholly responsible. This was the point made by Vladimir Bukovsky, a leading figure in the Soviet Human Rights Movement who, on being sentenced by a Soviet judge on a trumped-up charge, proudly declared, 'Do with me what you will—my freedom is inside of me.' He developed this theme further when, a few months after his release from the Soviet Union, in a speech in West Berlin he denounced the popular Western misconception that beyond the Berlin Wall are to be found the islands of the Gulag archipelago where oppression and violence begin, whereas on our side of the Wall there remains an undefiled ocean of freedom. 'In reality,' Bukovsky said, 'the frontiers of freedom and of slavery are much more complicated. They lie inside each one of us.' He went on to point out that millions in the East, despite persecution, torture and imprisonment in labour camps and psychiatric asylums are daily fighting for freedom by refusing to bow to the system, while in the West there are others who, by their mentality of sycophancy towards the totalitarian régimes, make themselves slaves. It is not enough to enjoy the benefits of living in a free society, there must be sufficient who believe strongly enough in that freedom to speak out for it and actively defend it.

It is not difficult to point to the defects and inadequacies in our 'free society'. It would be foolish to deny them. However, it would be even greater folly to assume that because we have not solved all the inherited historic problems of poor and squalid housing conditions, inadequate health care and poor standards of education in our schools, that there is something fundamentally wrong with our society and that we might possibly do better under some other system. Even the democratic system on which our free society is based is not without faults. There is no denying that it is an inefficient form of government—no doubt Mussolini was justified in his claim that he was able to make the railways run on time and the German *autobahn* network built by Hitler in the 1930s stands as evidence of efficiency of a sort. Furthermore, a democratic society can easily become a complacent society in which the people live insulated, as in a cotton-wool ball, from the harsh realities of the world by the fact that those who are supposed to exercise political leadership too often lack the courage to tell the truth, contenting themselves with licking their fingers to see which way the political wind is blowing so that they may curry favour with the electorate by telling the people what the pollsters report they wish to hear.

However the most fundamental charge that can be levelled against democracy—and it is one that is incontrovertible—is that it is, in the first resort, the weakest form of government that exists. The free society, by according as much liberty to its enemies as to its defenders, places powerful weapons in the hands of any politically motivated minority—however tiny—who seek to abuse its freedoms in pursuit of their totalitarian aims. The difficulties that Britain has experienced over a decade in countering the ruthless violence in Northern Ireland and the great industrial and political power wielded through the Trade Union movement and the Labour Party by individuals representing political philosophies wholly alien to the free society and to the aspirations of the British people, are but two examples of this.

As Churchill once observed in the House of Commons on 11 November 1947:

Nobody pretends that democracy is perfect or all-wise. Indeed it has been said that democracy is the worst form of government, except all those other forms that have been tried from time to time.

But if democracy is, in the *first* resort, a weak form of government it is also true that in the last resort it can be the strongest. So long as a people are kept in ignorance of the facts or, because of their unpleasant nature, are unwilling to face up to them, the free society is the weakest and most vulnerable. But once they have taken stock of a situation, once the path of honour, of duty and of salvation is clear, there is no limit to what a democracy, representing the resolve of a united people, will endure, will sacrifice and will achieve.

A characteristic of the free society is that it is only to be found in countries where capitalism or free enterprise flourish. This is no coincidence for capitalism—far from being a 'system' as it is so regularly and mistakenly called—is much closer to the natural condition of man, for it recognizes the individual's responsibility for his own and for his family's well-being and—provided that cartels and monopolies of capital and labour are restrained—is liable to provide for a diffusion of economic and political power throughout society. It is the antithesis of Socialism which seeks to establish a centralized bureaucratic system to regulate the lives and activities of its citizens.

By arrogating a monopoly of economic, industrial and political power to the State, Socialism strips the individual of all economic and political independence and ultimately of all personal liberty. The individual is deprived of freedom of choice on such matters as for whom he will work, to which union he will belong (or not belong), the kind of house he may live in, the form of education for his children, what he may read, what he may say and what he may do—until all independence and personal liberty become forfeit.

The free enterprise society rests on two justifications: it is better able to provide for the well-being and prosperity of the broad mass of the people and for their freedom. While not every capitalist society is a free society, it is an undisputed fact that where free enterprise is suppressed, no freedom remains.

The alternative to the free society is the totalitarian or closed society in which an individual or a narrow clique hold power without regard to the wishes or aspirations of the people, indeed frequently in defiance of them. Whatever ideals may have motivated them when they come to office or seize power, soon become corroded and corrupted by the abuse of power, wielded unashamedly to preserve in authority the new autocrats and to feather their own nests. Karl Marx would no doubt turn over in his Highgate grave if he knew the extent to which his misguided ideals had been perverted by those who claim to be his ideological followers. Soviet Communism (or Socialism as they prefer to call it) in no way seeks to run Russia in the interests of the masses, but rather in the interest of the governing elite. It is a little known fact that only 7% of the Soviet people are privileged enough to be admitted to membership of the Communist Party of the Soviet Union (CPSU). Party membership—the principal vehicle for self-advancement—is confined to those who in their school, in the Communist Youth League (KOMSOMOL), the Para-military Young Pioneers, or at their place of work, have demonstrated by their knowledge of Marxist dialectic and political activism in the Communist cause that they are worthy of such preferment.

The extent to which the Soviet Union is an egalitarian State may be judged by the fact that Party members who rise above a certain level in the hierarchy receive part of their salary in the form of coupons which give them access to *beryozkas*, foreign currency shops to which the ordinary Soviet citizen is denied access. Here the commissars and their wives can not only buy foreign consumer goods unavailable elsewhere in the Soviet Union, but can purchase for their family and friends the staples of diet at half or one-third the price paid by the ordinary citizen. A particular item sticks in my mind from my visit to the Soviet Union in 1974, when a two-kilo pack of sugar costing the ordinary citizen ninety kopek could be bought by the Party 'fat-cats' for thirty kopek—so much for the Socialist egalitarian society.

However, this creation of a self-perpetuating elite with after-tax differentials of pay infinitely greater between the surgeon and the hospital worker, the general and the private, the politician and the ordinary citizen, than anything to be found in the West, is by no means the most offensive aspect of the Socialist State. It is a society in which graft, corruption and inefficiency flourish but where all freedom and all means of self-expression or protest are ruthlessly repressed.

In the closed society it is a small step to move from the control and direction of capital to the control and direction of labour. Workers are told where they will work, what job they will do and what will be their conditions of employment, with no argument allowed. The trade unions instead of, as in the free society, being established to protect and further the interests of the workers, become instead the vehicle by which the State controls and disciplines the labour force. All strikes are illegal and, on the rare occasions when they occur, are ruthlessly repressed with the ringleaders earning hefty gaol sentences or consignment to psychiatric establishments. The basic human rights provided for under the Soviet constitution and by the Universal Declaration of Human Rights to which the Soviet Government is a signatory, are ignored. Those who seek to protest, to leave the country, or to secure the implementation of the Final Act of Helsinki to which, by a strange constitutional quirk, Mr Brezhnev in his capacity as Secretary-General of the CPSU (a position unknown to the Soviet constitution) pledged the faith of the Soviet Government, are hounded and terrorized by the KGB, the feared political police of the Communist Party.

All too frequently, those in the West who are ignorant of the history, the aims and the methods of Soviet Communism make the mistake of declaring, 'Well, let the Russians take over Africa, Asia or wherever—they will find themselves thrown out the way we were before them.' But that is to ignore one harsh fact of modern life: aided and abetted by modern technology in communications and weapons, there is almost no limit to the number of people who can be ruled by a small number of men, provided they are prepared to be ruthless enough. If the two hundred millions of peoples of Eastern and Central Europe—among the most politically and technologically advanced in the world—

remain under the Soviet tank-tracks more than thirty years after the end of the war, what hope is there for the Third World or indeed for Europe if the countervailing force of the NATO Alliance and its most prominent member, the United States, were no longer to be there to provide a balance and a choice for those who do not wish to fall into the Soviet orbit?

While there are those on the left of British politics, both in Parliament and in the Trade Union movement, who are politically sold-out to Moscow, there are also those who, while having no love of Moscow and no brief for the repression that exists under Socialism wherever it is to be found in practice today, genuinely believe that Socialism and Democracy can co-exist in a society. Indeed they have convinced themselves that there is something unique about British Socialism, that will avoid the excesses found elsewhere. They look down on the Russians, Chinese and East Europeans as being inferior peoples who have made a hash of Socialism.

However, British Socialists, such as Heffer, Foot and Benn, by some innate or God-given superiority, will be able to lead the British peoples towards the Socialist utopia with their democratic rights and freedoms intact. Those who fall for such a line truly deserve to lose their freedom. The fact is—and it is one that the protagonists of the Marxist–Socialist State refuse to admit—it is not only those who operate the system who are at fault, but the system itself. Socialism (as opposed to Social-Democracy) represents the antithesis of the freedom, human dignity and self-determination to which the vast majority of mankind aspires.

The Soviet Union's challenge to the West is three-fold: a growing military threat at both strategic and conventional levels, a military and economic assault against the Third World—as evidenced by recent Soviet involvement, direct and through third parties, in Africa—and a campaign of political subversion designed to undermine the Western democracies from within—the case of Portugal being merely the most flagrant so far.

While engaging the West for much of the 1970s in a diplomatic offensive known as 'detente', with the aim of persuading the Western democracies to lower their guard—a ploy in which they have been remarkably successful—the Soviet leadership simultaneously launched an all-out bid to achieve military supremacy over the West. The NATO allies, though outnumbered by the Soviets with a margin of between 2:1 and 3:1 in tanks, aircraft and manpower in Central Europe, have long drawn comfort from the clear superiority they have enjoyed in both tactical and strategic nuclear weapons, in the same way that the Victorian empire-builders, fighting superior numbers of Africans and Indians, took heart from the fact, immortalized by Belloc, that 'We have got the Maxim gun—and they have not!' Those days of effortless supremacy for the West are now gone. By a supreme effort, involving the diversion of vast economic and technological resources, the Soviets have taken the SALT (Strategic Arms Limitation Treaty) I Agreement of May 1972 as the opportunity to catch up with the United States and achieve parity or 'rough equivalence' in nuclear strike-power.

The Soviets now enjoy the psychological strength of no longer being the under-dog in the nuclear race and, by the same token, the United States, having lost its former clear advantage, may feel more wary of being involved in any future confrontation with the Soviets. Meanwhile in Europe the strengthening of Soviet conventional forces—more than one million Soviet soldiers with no fewer than 25,000 tanks now face Western Europe—has given the Soviet Union the capability of a 'standing start' attack, as was so dramatically achieved in Egypt and Syria against Israel on 6 October 1973. The Western allies, like Israel, base their defensive strategy on the mobilization of reservists and the deployment of reinforcements, but the recent development in Soviet strike capability means, according to the top military authorities in NATO, that the Alliance can now be sure of no more than seventy-two hours' warning—rather than the thirty days' warning or tension period previously relied upon.

Most worrying of all are the current trends in Soviet production. Soviet armaments factories are churning out 3,000/ 4,000 T-72 tanks, 1,800 combat aircraft and 250 nuclear missiles a year—out-building Britain's entire inventory every three months. Neither the restraint in arms-production shown by the West, nor the mood of 'detente', has in any way been reflected in an abatement in the arms-escalation policies of the Soviet Union.

Thus it must be the aim of the Western democracies to secure a serious and binding arms-control agreement with the Soviets. However, with the exception of an agreement not to deploy more than one anti-ballistic missile (ABM) system, little has been achieved in the SALT negotiations, and nothing at all in the talks on Mutual Balance Force Reductions (MBFR). In the absence of such an agreement, the NATO allies will have no choice but to make a seriously increased effort to strengthen their defences, for only in this way can it be brought home to the Soviet leadership that they are wasting their time—not to say their peoples' resources—through their arms-escalation policies and that they had best revert to the previous policies of peaceful co-existence that prevailed under Khruschev. If they do not, the nations of the Western Alliance will find themselves on the downwards path they have trodden with such disastrous results already once this century, a path on which the political options open to them will become more and more restricted until they reach the point of no return.

For too long the nations of Western Europe have taken a free ride off the United States and have neglected their own defences. If some three hundred million of the most prosperous and technologically capable peoples of the world are not prepared to make such modest sacrifices as are required to maintain their freedom, they will not long remain free, nor will they deserve to. Britain can play, if she so chooses, a key part in strengthening the cohesion and unity of Western Europe and can, by giving a good example to our European partners, strengthen Europe's defences so as to ensure that the deterrent is seen to be valid by those who may contemplate either war or military blackmail.

If we ignore the warnings, if we fail to confront the harsh realities that are before us, there is a danger that we will see peace, which we have taken so much for granted, slipping from our grasp. All too frequently it has been glibly asserted by politicians that the facts cannot be put before the people as they would be unpopular. I venture to believe that the overwhelming majority of the British people, when confronted with the facts, have enough common sense and moral fibre to recognize that there is, in the last resort, nothing more important to them than to continue to be able to live their lives in peace and in freedom. Only by arousing our people to the new dangers that confront them can we hope to turn the world away from the disaster course on which it is set. If we can achieve this, there can be no doubt that the strengths and values of the free society will prove more enduring that the ideologies of the totalitarian police-states which give the appearance of being all powerful but which are rotten to the core and will ultimately be overthrown by their own peoples demanding liberation—provided only that the Western democracies are able to keep the torch of freedom burning brightly.

Narindar Saroop

Freedom and Race

In the year 1290 King Edward I of England sought to enhance his popularity by expelling the Jews from his realm. Over six centuries later Adolf Hitler used anti-Semitism as a key weapon in the Nazi (National Socialist) Party's fight to achieve power. His final monument is the broken gas chambers of Auschwitz and the other extermination camps. The pogroms of Tsarist Russia have been replaced by new forms of persecution, called anti-Zionism, under the Soviet régime. But anti-Semitism is but one form of racialism.

Racialism, both as a social phenomenon and a political weapon, has a global history. Its continued existence on a world scale was massively documented in 1975 by The Foundation for the Studies of Plural Societies.[1] It existed in classical antiquity. It was exemplified in the story of the Good Samaritan in the New Testament.[2] It was writ large in both the history of the Indian sub-continent and in the attitude of the Chinese Middle Kingdom to the 'barbarians' without. It was manifested in the attitudes of many people in the imperial powers of Western Europe to the inhabitants of their colonial possessions and this, ironically, was matched by the attitude of many Japanese to Koreans. In the 1970s it is possible to circle the globe from Indonesia via the still partly tribal African continent (not only South Africa with its system of apartheid) to the Americas, and at all points the problem continues to exist and in so doing provides a major threat to stability and peace both domestically and internationally.

The appeal and, often, the successful political exploitation of racial doctrines—even though the evidence from the biological sciences disproves them—has led many of the finest minds of each century to challenge them. None did this with greater courage and success than the author of *Robinson Crusoe*:

In 1689, as a result of the Glorious Revolution and having accepted the Declaration of Right, William and Mary became King and Queen of England. Later that year the Bill of Rights joined the Magna Carta as the enshrinement of those liberties which the coming generations of the British peoples were to be privileged to enjoy. Nevertheless there was a mixture of political forces which were opposed to the Settlement, the new monarchy and the general pattern of development in Britain. In the following decade they never ceased to exploit the fact that Mary's William was Dutch. At the turn of the century Daniel Defoe wrote:

During this time came out an abhorred pamphlet, in very ill verse, written by one Mr. Tutchin, and called The Foreigners, in which the author, who he was I then knew not, fell personally upon the King, then upon the Dutch nation, and, after having reproached his majesty with crimes that his worst enemies could not think of without horror, he sums up all in the odious name FOREIGNER.

Defoe who occupies a place second to none in the history of British freedom fighters, to use a term which is only too often distorted and perverted today, riposted in words which still speak to us:[3]

> The Romans first with Julius Caesar came,
> Including all the nations of that name,
> Gauls, Greeks, and Lombards; and by computation,
> Auxiliaries or slaves of ev'ry nation.
> With Hengist, Saxons; Danes with Sweno came,
> In search of plunder, not in search of fame.
> Scots, Picts, and Irish from th' Hibernian shore;
> And Conquering William brought the Normans o'er.
>
> Dutch Walloons, Flemings, Irishmen, and Scots,
> Vandois, and Valtolines, and Huguenots,
> In good queen Bess's charitable reign,
> Supplied us with three hundred thousand men;
> Religion, —God, we thank ye! sent them hither,

Priests, protestants, the devil, and all together;
Of all professions, and of ev'ry trade,
All that were persecuted or afraid.

Thus from a mixture of all kinds began,
That heterogeneous thing, an Englishman.

Defoe's powerful onslaught may have both enhanced his greatness and strengthened those who opposed racialism but most certainly it did not lead to the disappearance of racialism in Britain. Indeed, in Britain, as in all other countries with a mixed population, racialism has remained a problem until the present day, as has its exploitation for political purposes. In the boom period of the Railway Age there was widespread prejudice against the Irish navvies who actually undertook so much of the construction work. It is ironic to note that in recent years the words 'Black Irish' have been used as a pejorative term for West Indian immigrants! At the turn of the century there was strong antagonism especially in London and a number of other major cities, to the Jewish refugees from Tsarist Russia.

The anti-Semitism of the years between the two World Wars, especially that connected with Oswald Mosley's British Union of Fascists, has been well documented. What has been largely neglected was the success of the Communist Party, especially among the youth and Jewish youth in particular, in presenting itself as the true anti-Fascist party and friend of the Jewish people. It is only necessary to recall the Nazi-Soviet Pact of 1939 and the persecution of Jews in the USSR in order to expose the falsity of those claims. Even the Polish Forces, whose pilots fought with such gallantry in the Battle of Britain and elsewhere, were not free from slander. On this occasion the attack was from the Marxist left which at one end of the scale nick-named West Cromwell Road, Kensington the 'Polish Corridor' (of course, with many brothels and as a centre of the war-time black market) and at the other end of the scale attacked these allies of ours as 'Fascists'. This was because they were Polish patriots who were fighting to regain their freedom and national independence and who had no wish that the sacrifices they were making in the common effort to destroy the Hitler régime should result, as sadly it did in the end, in their country being enslaved by a Stalinist-controlled government.

In the years since 1945, and particularly so in the last decade, the target of the racialists in Britain has been the Asian and West Indian immigrant communities. It is an alarming feature of British society that by the year 1977 the National Front was the fourth largest political party in the country and showed signs of becoming the third largest within a measurable space of time unless some countervailing philosophy came into action. But if this dangerous trend is to be reversed the first prerequisite is an understanding of the nature of race and racialism.

Whilst it is true that the evidence from the biological sciences demonstrates that the human race is one—a total whole—it is equally true that races differ enormously in their cultures, histories, languages, traditions and appearance. The diversity between peoples matches the diversity which is to be found among individuals of a single race. Every field of human achievement demonstrates diversity. Why have the English produced a great literature, the Dutch great painting and the Japanese a uniquely delicate art? Why are athletes from certain parts of Africa such outstanding Olympic runners? Why have the Jews produced such a wealth of great performing musicians and world-class chess players out of all proportion to their numbers? The list of such questions is endless and no two answers would be the same in any sense of a mechanical comparison. What remains is the common lot of birth, life and death. To this the genius of Shakespeare gave the answer.

Hath not a Jew eyes? hath not a Jew hands, organs, dimensions, senses, affections, passions! fed with the same food, hurt with the same weapons, subjected to the same diseases, healed by the same means, warmed and cooled by the same winter and summer, as a Christian is? If you prick us, do we not bleed? If you tickle us, do we not laugh? If you poison us, do we not die? and if you wrong us, shall we not revenge?

(*The Merchant of Venice*, Act III, scene 1.)

The appeal to compassion, humanity and tolerance should,

nevertheless, not be permitted to obscure the fundamental problem of the relationship between hereditary and environmental influences on individuals, groups and peoples—a relationship which is not susceptible to precise quantification. Indeed one of the current threats to freedom is the standpoint of those 'scientists' who regard the assumption of equal inherited ability as something which does not require experimental evidence to establish it and which it is positively wicked to question because the conclusion might disagree with their social and political preconceptions. Paradoxically not only does this standpoint assist racialists (the old cry in the US of 'nigger-lover') but it also hampers intelligent policy formation because it inhibits research into these complex and sensitive areas and thus weakens the development of the base from which realistic social policies could be formulated.[4]

Nevertheless racialist politics in the streets are far removed from the sciences even if the sciences are used for purposes of justification. Equally, they are far removed, save for the purpose of emotional exploitation, from differences in colour, dress and culinary customs. At rock bottom racialist politics spring from the fundamental factor of the real world which is that resources are always relatively scarce in relation to human desires and expectations. Resources can be distributed and used in alternate patterns. In stark terms this means that there will be competition for jobs, housing, education, health services and other social benefits. The higher the level of unemployment, the more acute the housing shortage, the longer the waiting time for hospital treatment, the greater the gulf between good and bad schools and the greater the lack of other social benefits, the greater the opportunity for racialists to create and exploit communal friction.

Britain in the 1970s with her economic stagnation and uncertainty of political and social purpose presents a classic situation in which intelligent, immoral and ruthless political operators can exploit the fears and prejudices of sections of the white population, especially the most ignorant and unthinking members of it. Attitudes are exacerbated in areas of high immigrant concentration especially when thus combined with an inadequate supply of facilities. The defeat of racialist politics in Britain will only be possible if the country's economic and general political problems are successfully tackled. Of course education has an enormous and vital role to play but historical experience shows that on its own, however valuable, it is always in danger of falling into the role of pious preaching.

The statements and activities of such an organization as the National Front speak for themselves and require no exhaustive comment. What does demand analysis is the role of the different varieties of Marxists who proclaim themselves to be the true friends and champions of the so-called immigrant community, and in so doing make a deliberate play for all that is best and most idealistic in the white youth of the country, as well as seeking mass recruitment among the immigrant youth.

The record of Marxist régimes, as exemplified by Soviet persecution not only of Jews but of Ukrainian nationalists and the smaller peoples of the Caucasus, to name only some examples, as well as the treatment of the Tibetans by Maoist China, demonstrates Marxism in practice when it has achieved power and condemns itself. But what of the Marxists in Britain? Are they different? On 13 August 1977 the Marxists, allegedly demonstrating against the National Front in the South London Borough of Lewisham, elected to fight a pitched battle against the police in which they used such weapons as ammonia, coshes, glass bottles, knives and pepper. They claimed that the police were protecting the National Front and thus justified cries of 'Kill, kill!' when a policeman fell to the ground.[5] But only a few days earlier they had used similar tactics and methods outside the Grunwick factory in North London in the course of an industrial dispute, in which 243 policemen were injured. Their self-proclaimed mission is to destroy existing British society and to that end they preach total class-hatred with a paranoic savagery. They seek violent confrontation for its own sake as they believe that this heightens the class-consciousness and class-hatred of the proletariat. Similarly they seek to enrol and exploit members of the immigrant community in their drive to establish a Marxist totalitarian state in Britain. Both Marxists and Fascists use racialist politics for the same reason, even if from different angles.

In this situation it is somewhat salutary to read one of the first Policy Statements issued by The National Association for Freedom shortly after its foundation. In a document entitled 'All the Queen's subjects' it declared:

We believe that in return for the duty of personal allegiance to the Sovereign, citizens enjoy the right to be governed by the laws and customs of this realm, duly enforced without fear or favour.

The right to live under the Queen's peace is being endangered by a rise in racial tension and the beginnings of racial violence. In the present period of acute and worsening economic conditions, there are ruthless political movements which are seeking to exploit racial differences by appeals to envy, fear, greed and ignorance.

On the one hand the Fascists of the National Front and the British National Party seek to achieve political power by stirring up racial hatred against the Queen's immigrant subjects. They are increasingly active in localities with a high immigrant population.

They are now increasing their propaganda in factories and other work places. On the other hand the Communist Party, the International Socialists, Maoists and other Marxists even as they preach unbridled class hatred, parade themselves as the champions of the immigrants against the Fascist danger and as the true defenders of racial equality.

They are conducting competitive propaganda and recruiting drives in factories and elsewhere aimed not only at the immigrant youth but also at all that is most idealistic, compassionate and tolerant in the native-born British youth. It is necessary to remember how in the 1930s the Communists won so much support, particularly among students and Christian youth, both for themselves as a party and for Stalin's Russia, by posing as the most anti-Nazi force.

The National Association for Freedom declares that these organisations, Fascists and Marxist alike, are the enemies of Freedom. They exploit the present economic and social conditions for their own political purposes which would, if either triumphed, result in the setting up of a one party totalitarian dictatorship.

The National Association for Freedom therefore calls on its members, supporters and friends to oppose these twin evils with all the energy they can command. In so doing it declares that a British citizen is not to be judged by his race, colour or creed but by his devotion and adherence to British Freedom. The non-British are those totalitarians, both Fascists and Marxists, who seek to destroy British Freedom. The role of the National Association for Freedom is to help unite all citizens irrespective of race, colour and creed in defence of Freedom and against all forms of totalitarianism.

The National Association for Freedom invites all men and women who cherish Freedom to join its ranks and help to defend it.

Policy statements, however praiseworthy, are insufficient on their own. The proof of the pudding is always in the eating. This means that two further questions demand consideration. The first is the position and attitude of the immigrants themselves. The second, closely related question, is the attitude and actions of the mass of the British people, the so-called silent majority.

If in what follows there appears to be an undue concentration on the Asian immigrant community, it is not only because this is where the writer has the greatest experience and knowledge but also because, of all the groups of racial immigrants since World War II, e.g. Poles, Hungarians, etc., they form the largest ethnic group. Further, by their inherent characteristics such as individual enterprise, thrift, love and cohesion of the family unit they provide the greatest potential in contributing to the maintenance of a free society in Britain. Precisely because of this they also provide the most attractive target for the Marxists, particularly in the next few years, when the process of harmonious assimilation is still incomplete, and when the next generation has to face additional and unusual stresses and strains; but more of this later.

Until recently immigration into Britain has been for reasons of religious and political refuge. Economic reasons and the large number that have come in because of them are essentially a new phenomenon. This point is worth making because the coloured immigrant is therefore likely to be as complacent, if not more so, as the average Englishman to the cry 'Freedom is in Danger'. On the contrary the average Pole or Hungarian in Britain is much more likely to appreciate the precious and unique quality of freedom in the United Kingdom. This is not to say that the average Asian immigrant has little knowledge of freedom—quite the contrary. Notwithstanding the vicissitudes of history over the centuries, the Sikh and the Pakistani (forming the overwhelming majority of the Asian immigrant community) are inherently individualistic and have fought for generations to preserve religious freedom as well as individuality within an overall framework. Nevertheless their primary reasons for coming to Britain were economic and not political or religious. As far as West Indian immigrants are concerned it needs to be stressed that when they came to Britain they felt they were coming to their second homeland to live under the rule of their Queen. Such were their expectations.

Successive British governments, far from stemming the flow of immigration, encouraged it as a means of securing much-needed labour, whether in the form of doctors and nurses in the Health Service or in the manning of the transport system and the textile industry. At that stage they had little thought of the limited geographical size and natural resources in Britain, let alone of the possibility of the economic recession which was to develop in the 1970s. Given the British traditions of tolerance, equality before the law and freedom they had no doubt that a stable multi-racial society could be established. Present-day realities make that an infinitely more difficult task.

There is a popular psychological theory that, if shipwrecked, a human being instinctively adopts the following sequence—need for shelter, desire for food (or vice versa), desire for companionship and the need for social acceptance. Using this analogy it might be argued that the Asian community is at the beginning of the stage where the desire for social acceptance is of paramount importance.

There have been endless arguments about integration and/or assimilation. To a realist this appears to be very much an academic argument and a semantic one at that. Nevertheless some of the more vociferous immigrant leaders and their fellow-travelling whites regard both integration and assimilation as dirty words. They maintain that there is a ring of coercion about them and imply that the immigrant communities are in danger of losing their individual cultures and identities. This is a dubious argument, particularly as far as the young are concerned. How many of the immigrant youth, as opposed to their elders, would wish to maintain a separate cultural identity? How many of them would be able to withstand the pressures from whatever way of life is being practised by their contemporaries in the overall community at large?

Sadly it has to be recognized that national cultures are tending to break down all over the world with a uniform pop and Coca-Cola culture extending its grip. This applies, for example, to large sections of youth in the Indian sub-continent. Why should the situation in Britain be different? One of the questions which exercises older Asians in the immigrant community, who donate much of their savings to build mosques and temples, is what will be the future of these buildings? How many will use them in the future? Is the money really being spent for the benefit of the next generation? Equally large problems present themselves when one turns to such matters as marriage and social customs. Many immigrant youths are torn two ways. There is the pull of affection and discipline towards the family and tradition. There is the pull of British society dragging them in an opposite direction. The picture is one of the hold of religion diminishing and the family unit breaking down. The decline of these two powerful sources of moral and spiritual succour will not be compensated for by the ability of the next generation to speak the patois of Bradford or Southall, or whatever version of English is being spoken in their particular area. An understanding of these tensions is as important as is an understanding of white anxieties for those who concern themselves with the problem of race.

One of the essences of freedom is that it allows diversity in groups, permits individuals to be different. England has traditionally always welcomed diversity in life, and the ideal situation would be one in which the immigrant community takes an increasing part in the full social, cultural and political life of the country, does not remain aloof, can and should conform in a broad, loose way to 'what the Romans do' but without losing its own distinctive culture. In this connection it must be mentioned that, because of the concentration of immigrants in certain parts of the country, their voting power is now decisive in between thirty and forty Parliamentary constituencies. There are encouraging signs that large numbers of immigrants are beginning to feel that they should play a role through the traditional British democratic processes. But this still leaves unanswered the key question of how to overcome the very real doubts and fears which exist in both host and immigrant communities and thus to prevent the expansion of racialist politics.

History shows that it has been the teachings of the great religions combined with the processes of education that has enabled much of mankind to advance from barbarism to civilization. Parallel to this, legislation and the rule of law underpinned the development of stable political societies. It is for this reason that it is foolish automatically to criticize racial legislation or to argue that it always does more harm than good. There is a strong case for a limited amount of racial legislation to act as a guide to public opinion and behaviour. However, both it and its implementation need to be carried out in such a way so that whilst helping the immigrant community it does not provide grounds for Fascist propaganda to argue that sections of the white population are being discriminated against in their turn and are becoming second-class citizens. This needs to be understood as a difficult area. Even more difficult is the area of what might only too truly be described as the Race Relations Industry. Some examples may be revealing.

Many race relations organizations have been penetrated by Marxists and their fellow travellers. Their approach is a purely ideological one and they seek to exclude anyone who does not share their views. There was the case when one of the Inner London Boroughs was interviewing applicants for the vacant post of Community Relations Officer. One of the applicants, realistic, able and with overseas experience felt that the general tenor of questions by the Selection Committee was markedly left wing. It was obvious to him that he was not going to be considered for the job, particularly when he was asked what he would do in the case of a confrontation between the police and a crowd of black people. He replied that he would ask the crowd to disperse peacefully and suggest other ways in which they could make their grievances known. This answer was greeted by a horrified silence and the candidate was advised by one of the Selection Committee that he appeared to be 'unacceptably in favour of authority'. Another example, this time from Southampton, where a distinguished individual in his late forties was repeatedly rebuffed by the local Community Relations Council when he sought to do some work in this field. Undoubtedly among his handicaps and disqualifications were the facts that he had spent twenty years in India, spoke two Indian languages fluently and really knew the people among whom he wished to work.

Whilst a consideration of the causes of racialism and a discussion of legal and organizational measures can be helpful it does not for one second remove the simple fact that racial harmony will triumph or be defeated in the homes, streets and neighbourhoods. I would like to conclude this brief essay on a note of personal experience. In July 1976 a Sikh youth was murdered in Southall. As a result and because of acts of provocation by the National Front in that area, mass meetings were held in many Sikh Temples around London in some of which I was invited to participate. In one case several hundred people attended, including a cadre of West Indian and white Marxists who endeavoured to take over the proceedings. When I spoke to my own people in Punjabi this cadre attempted to howl me down shouting that I was an ex-officer and a businessman. Because of language difficulties many of the Sikh elders had some difficulty in following those parts of the proceedings which were taken up with resolutions moved by this largely imported vociferous minority and thus conducted in English. After the meeting I stressed to them the dangers they would run into if they allowed themselves to be taken over by the Marxists. They replied 'We are not fools, we know what they want, we know they wish to use us. But what can we do? They are the only whites who are supporting us against the National Front.'

This is the essence of the challenge to the silent majority of the British people. It is true that the immigrants have to adjust and acclimatize to the British way of life. But it is even more true that the belief that 'it can never happen here' is the most dangerous belief which people can hold when their society is being undermined and challenged by totalitarian forces. The problem of race in Britain is and will remain probably the single most important issue in British society in the immediate years. Those who seek to defend freedom cannot stand aside. Freedom can be destroyed, as it was in Germany in the 1930s, by racial politics. Every citizen, whether in pub or football ground, in dance hall or on public transport, faces a daily challenge not to stand on one side but actively to promote racial harmony. Freedom is indeed indivisible. The freedom that has to be defended is the common property of both whites and immigrants. It is a joint and binding duty to defend it.

1   William A. Veenhoven (ed.): *Case Studies on Human Rights and Fundamental Freedoms—A World Survey*, Vols 1 & 2, Martinus Nijhoff, The Hague 1975
2   Luke, Chapter 10, verses 25–37
3   Daniel Defoe: *The True-Born Englishman* 1700/01
4   For an extremely important discussion of the problem, see Sir Andrew Huxley, FRS: *Evidence, Clues and Motive in Science*—the 1977 Presidential Address to the British Association; *The Times* leading article 1 September 1977 and the article by its science correspondent Mr Pearce Wright
5   See the *Sunday Telegraph* of 14 August 1977, and other newspapers

Dr K. W. Watkins

The Challenge to Freedom

'Sir, we know our will is free, and there's an end on't.'

(BOSWELL'S *Life of Johnson*, vol. 1, p. 82)

Man's long and far from completed march from barbarism to civilization has rested on the existence of free will and the growth of freedom in which to exercise it. Advanced twentieth-century man regards himself, with some justification, as having left behind shamans and witch doctors, societies scarred by human sacrifice and the galaxy of superstitions which burdened his ancestors. Yet twentieth-century man has also experienced or witnessed some of the most brutal and repressive dictatorships known to history. Science and technology have been shown not to be neutral forces in the world of politics but forces that can be used for or against freedom. A distinction, however, must be made between authoritarian régimes in which, however savage the repression, an individual can still think for himself, even if he then acts at his utmost peril, and totalitarian régimes which seek total control not only of the present but of future generations through the process of indoctrination and brainwashing. It was the Communists who long ago coined the slogan 'the battle of ideas' and they were right to do so, for in society men act according to their beliefs. Today the great challenge to freedom is in the realm of ideas. The purpose of this essay is to try to examine the nature of the challenge at a theoretical level and then to examine its practical significance in two specific fields.

Whereas it is a fundamental tenet of liberal political thought that in a dynamic and changing world man cannot expect to arrive at the completely correct answers, Marxism, on the contrary, claims to be a science. When a series of possible solutions to a scientific problem are postulated only one of them can be correct. Engels, in the course of his oration at Marx's graveside, declared:[1]

Just as Darwin discovered the law of evolution in organic nature, so Marx discovered the law of evolution in human history.

Lenin wrote:[2]

The Marxian doctrine is omnipotent because it is true.

Over the decades each successive Communist dictator has ensured that his lackeys have proclaimed him to be the greatest Marxist or Marxist–Leninist of his time. Three examples will suffice.

Of Stalin, Voroshilov wrote:[3]

Comrade Stalin is the great continuator of the work of Lenin. Comrade Stalin is the Lenin of to-day. Comrade Stalin is the genius of Socialism. Comrade Stalin is the great architect of Communism.

Of Mao, Lin Piao, whilst he was heir apparent, wrote:[4]

Comrade Mao Tse-tung is the greatest Marxist–Leninist of our era.

Of Kim Il Sung, the North Korean dictator, his controlled press frequently writes as:[5]

The greatest Marxist–Leninist and the outstanding leader of the times who creates history.

The innocent dismiss such uncritical adulation as emotional propaganda designed to underpin the political legitimacy of the particular dictator. They fail to recognize that it is the claim to the 'scientific' inheritance which is being established. The more sophisticated ask why it is when so many of the predictions of Marx and Lenin have failed to materialize that the establishment of this 'scientific' legitimacy is regarded as all-important.

Among the predictions of Marx that have failed to materialize was that of the 'increasing misery of the working class' in industrial societies. It was the result of his failure to foresee the development of mass political democracy, the great enlargement of the middle class, the growth of modern trade unions and, above all, the impact of escalating technological innovation and application. Marxists attempt to evade this difficulty in several ways. Some admit that Marx, being human, erred on the time-scale and the rate and pattern of development. Others twist what was originally an economic argument and proceed to argue that even if the material well-being of the masses has improved this is more than off-set by the psychological suffering and deprivation to which capitalism subjects the workers. Yet others go so far as to admit that there are definite errors in the Marxist classics but claim that such errors do not invalidate the fundamental correctness of Marxism. This development is not only important but provides a key to the battle of ideas.

Particularly over the last decade, especially in academic life, a new growth Marxist industry has developed. There are those who seek to establish by textual analysis that Marx was essentially right but that it was Engels who made major errors in his own works and also in his editing of some of Marx's manuscripts. Others have seized upon the recently available writings of the young and student Marx and make great play of the differences to be found between the young Marx and the old Marx. Yet others claim that Marxism, despite the errors of Marx himself, is scientifically correct. A leading exponent of this last school is the American Marxist authority and scholar, Michael Harrington, who has written:[6]

Both Marx and Engels then contributed to the distortion of Marxism, the former on occasion, the latter more systematically. But if these misstatements were, particularly in the case of Marx, only episodic and counterbalanced by a huge corpus of intellectual work that put matters rightly, why was the false coin of Marxism so widely accepted and the genuine treasure all but ignored.

At the end of the same chapter:

So, for most people the first step in grasping the new and future Marx is to forget everything they have heard or read about the familiar Marx. At the same time, they must accept one of history's strangest ironies: that Marx and the Marxists made a major contribution to the misunderstanding of Marxism.

A simple man might feel drawn to the conclusion that a greater irony is that a writer like Harrington—and there are many others—is so confident that he knows, better than Marx, what Marx meant to write or should have written but failed to write. The catch in this game is revealed by the first part of the book's title: *The Twilight of Capitalism.* As with Stalin, Mao and Kim Il Sung, Harrington and those scholars like him are seeking to inherit the 'science'. In reality and practical terms this means the theory of the inevitability of the revolutionary overthrow of capitalism—i.e. of pluralist societies which form the base for individual freedom—the doctrine of class struggle and class hatred, and the inevitability of the Socialist society in the form in which they, the true Marxists, conceive it. It is all in the mainstream of intellectual totalitarianism. At this stage free will has been abandoned. All is sacrificed to the faith that there is a 'science' of Marxism which holds the key to the future and is the guarantee of future human happiness. The end justifies the means. The mind is shuttered and is impervious to counter-argument or criticism.

If this seems too strong an assertion it is easy to refer to the development of dissidence in the USSR and East Europe. There are those like Solzhenitsyn and Bukovsky who reached the stage, after years of painful analysis as well as physical suffering, at which they could ask themselves whether the fundamental principles of Marxism were correct.

Solzhenitsyn reached the conclusion that the terror of the 1930s was not merely Stalinist but was both started by Lenin and was inherent in the philosophical system. For a Soviet citizen this was an enormous feat. Not to reach the same conclusion is, for the citizen of a free society, a feat of historical and political illiteracy for such a citizen has for years been able to read in official Soviet publications about the establishment of 'The All-Russian Extraordinary Commission' (Vecheka) in 1918 under the leadership of the Polish aristocrat and Bolshevik, Felix Dzerzhinsky. This body was the forerunner of the NKVD, today's KGB and was the official instrument of the Red Terror.[7] What is difficult but essential to appreciate is how there are still dissidents who, despite incredible suffering, believe that Marxism is correct but has been perverted in the USSR. They, unlike citizens of a free society, have been subjected to brainwashing from the cradle.

In a very real sense Marxism can be considered as a secular religion. The theology is historical materialism, the warring Communists, Trotskyists and Maoists are schismatic churches, the deviationists are heretics and the Party Control Commission is the equivalent of the Inquisition. These parallels have been drawn before but are none the worse for repetition. No other statement arouses such fury in Marxists—are they not dialectical materialists, atheists, anti-metaphysical and are they not followers of scientific Socialism? What is emphasized here is the claim to science. Where there is a difference of opinion, the opposing comrade is being bourgeois or non-scientific or undialectical or mechanical. The list of charges and counter charges is endless but each contendant, whether individual or party, is convinced that he understands the 'science' and is applying it correctly and since it is a science there is only one correct solution for each strategic and tactical problem that arises. This is the basis of the bitterness and hatred with which feuding Marxists confront one another. It has a particular relevance to the phenomenon of Euro-Communism.

At this moment liberals are being lulled by statements such as that made by Marchais, the General Secretary of the French Communist Party, that 'the theory of the dictatorship of the proletariat' is no longer relevant to French conditions. Similarly journalists and politicians write and speak about the so-called moderates in post-Maoist China. They neglect two factors in so doing. The first is that Lenin repeatedly taught that the road to political power was not a straight one but that real Marxist revolutionaries had to prepare for twists and turns, advances and retreats, and had to, as necessary, manoeuvre and lie in order to deceive and defeat the class enemy. It was all summed up in the

apophthegm of the old Bolshevik, Yaroslavsky: 'Whatever coincides with the interests of the Proletarian Revolution is ethical.' The debate is one about strategy and tactics, not about
fundamental aims. It is not the true test of whether Communism
is changing.

Secondly, for Communist parties to change fundamentally as
opposed to superficially it would mean that debate would have to
be possible over the validity of the fundamental Marxist theoretical model. No such debates are on record. In practical terms it
would have to mean the end of the practice of 'democratic centralism' as the basis of Communist party organization and the
recognition of the rights of factions within a Communist party.
The whole theory of democratic centralism was worked out by
Lenin in 1904.[8] It has remained unchallenged to this day in
every Communist party. Communist parties will veer in their relations with Social Democrats, Liberals and others but within
the Party the iron discipline is maintained. Change is only possible as the result of one faction destroying another in the top
leadership and then the victors are always the true Marxists;
'scientists', who have overcome the traitors, anti-Marxists, non-
scientists. Anyone doubting this might well study the in-fighting
in the Chinese Communist Party over the last decade and a half
and then compare it with the factional struggles in the USSR
during the twenties and thirties.

With such a history of both theory and practice it is logical to
ask why Marxism continues to have such an appeal for some of
those who are privileged to live in a free society. The answer, it is
suggested, is multi-faceted. Man, an imperfect species living in
an imperfect world, still, despite all his advance, lives under the
shadows of the threat of war, economic instability with its attendant inflation and unemployment, racial conflict in many
areas, and with poverty and suffering for many millions. Any
compassionate human being must be moved by the plight of so
many of his fellow men. Marxism claims to be the science which
can demonstrate that all these evils arise from the existing social
system and will be abolished in the new Socialist society. It is the
prospect of a relatively short cut to the earthly paradise that
appeals together with the easy identification of the causes of the

evils in the shape of the bourgeoisie and its capitalist system. Thus the appeal is made to idealism and compassion on the one hand and to hatred of a definable enemy on the other. (The political importance of hatred was well understood by Adolf Hitler.) Next in a world in which, in many so-called advanced countries, religion has been substantially undermined, Marxism offers a new faith for those in search of one. A third, and by no means the least important, reason is the failure of those who live in free societies to cry aloud the achievements of those societies. It is not a question of denying the gross imperfections of our world but of stressing again and again—and all the evidence is there—the achievements which have been wrought century by century and decade by decade as man has struggled to his present position. In other words, it is necessary to fight Marxism in the battle of ideas. Those who confine themselves to party programmes, winning elections and gaining office, and to the processes of government and administration, labour in vain if they fail to understand that all such activities only have meaning and importance to the extent that they take place within a conscious framework of the defence of freedom.

At this stage it is possible to consider the battle of ideas in the two key areas which will essentially decide the future. The first is education and the second is industry. In the former, minds are shaped. In the latter, there occurs the crucial political struggle.

The creation of what is called 'class consciousness' has always been at the heart of Marxist teaching and remains so today. That is why Marxists devote so much time and energy to education, from primary school to university, and to establishing control over the printed and spoken word. Marx and Engels (and later Lenin) repeatedly stressed the unity of theory and practice in the creation of a new consciousness.[9]

For the production on a mass scale of this communist consciousness, and for the success of the cause itself, the alteration of men on a mass scale is necessary, an alteration which can only take place in a practical movement, *a revolution*; this revolution is necessary, therefore, not only because the ruling class cannot be overthrown in any other way, but also because the class *overthrowing* it can only in a revolution succeed in ridding itself of all the muck of ages and become fitted to found society anew.

In a basic Soviet text, M. I. Kalinin, President of the USSR observed:[10]

In my opinion education is the definite, purposeful and systematic influencing of the mind of the person being educated in order to imbue him with the qualities desired by the educator. It seems to me that such a definition broadly covers all that we put into the concept of education, such as instilling a definite world outlook, morality and rules of human intercourse, fashioning definite traits of character and will, habits and tastes, development of physical qualities, etc.

Stalin's cultural hatchet-man, A. A. Zhdanov, laid down a clear cultural line for the faithful:[11]

We demand that our comrades, both practising writers and those in positions of literary leadership, should be guided by that without which the Soviet order cannot live, that is to say, by politics, so that our young people may be brought up not in the spirit of do-nothing and don't care, but in an optimistic revolutionary spirit.

and Mao Tse-Tung found time to ensure:[12]

... that literature and art fit well into the whole revolutionary machine as a component part, that they operate as powerful weapons for uniting and educating the people and for attacking and destroying the enemy, and that they help the people to fight the enemy with one heart and one mind.

Of course these dogmatic tenets which have been and still are instilled into the faithful in party training schools are modified when the party, and its intellectuals, seek to win allies and influence people among Social Democrats, Liberals, Christians and others. It is here that the 'Front or Broad' organizations play a role whether it is in the form of a Christian-Marxist dialogue, of uniting 'Scientists for Peace' or in cultural fields such as 'progressive theatre'. The history of international Communism is littered not only with the names of willing and conscious fellow travellers, like the late Dean of Canterbury and D. N. Pritt in England but with those of thousands of intellectuals who at one stage or another were sucked into broad organizations only either to be spewed out later or to make a break when they came to realize the true nature of the organization to which they had permitted themselves.

The unfortunate ones, of course, were those who were liquidated when Marxist power had been established and their eyes were open too late. That these objectives and tactics are still being pursued in the 1970s has been fully documented in a recent study by a group of British scholars.[13]

What needs to be stressed is that this offensive can only be countered when there is a clear understanding of the magnitude of the threat it presents. Those who pretend either that it does not exist (ignoring the evidence) or that it is relatively unimportant are in fact playing into the hands of those who seek to subvert free societies.

It is, however, in industry, at what Marx termed 'the point of production' that Marxists believe that the key political struggle takes place. According to their theoretical model the capitalist class extracts surplus value (the source of capitalist profit) from the workers in the process of production. It is thus for them a 'scientific' fact that under capitalism there *cannot* be such a thing as a just (fair) wage. They conveniently forget two points. The first is that in any society there must be savings, i.e. forgone consumption, if there is to be investment and future economic growth. This process must take place whether the mechanism be that of a mixed economy or a centrally controlled one. The second point they forget is, who, in a complex and technologically advanced society, will in fact administer the economy on behalf of the workers when private ownership of the means of production has been eliminated. When challenged on this point they seek refuge from it by a nonstop incantation of the word 'participation'. They ignore the reality of the vast discrepancies in living standards between the elites and the masses in Communist states.

The real difference of course is that in the market economy, economic pluralism provides the basis for political pluralism and the maintenance of freedom. In the centrally controlled economy the possession of monopoly economic power is the base for monopoly political power (the two are but different sides of the same coin) and with it the disappearance of individual freedom, a process which is sustained by ideological indoctrination.

Those industrialists and businessmen who believe that it is possible to buy off Marxists are staggering down a well known historical path. Declining Rome sought to buy off Alaric and his Goths. Weakened Saxon Britain paid Danegeld without avail until Alfred built his fleet. This is not to deny that there is conflict of interest in industry and that in a free society there will always be wage bargaining and clashes of interest.

The point is made to emphasize the difference in attitude towards the trade unions that exists between an old-fashioned worker, however militant, and the Marxists who seek to exploit the unions for revolutionary ends. This, too, is founded in the theoretical literature from the time of Marx and Engels onwards. Well over a century ago Engels wrote:[14]

These strikes, at first skirmishes, sometimes result in weighty struggles; they decide nothing it is true, but they are the strongest proof that the decisive battle between the bourgeoisie and the proletariat is approaching. *They are the school of war of the working men in which they prepare themselves for the great struggle which cannot be avoided . . . And as schools of war they are unexcelled.*

He was developing a theme of Marx where the latter wrote:[15]

Trades Unions work well as centres of resistance against the encroachment of capital. They fail partly from an injudicious use of their power. They fail generally from limiting themselves to a guerrilla struggle against the effects of the system, instead of simultaneously trying to change it, instead of using their organised forces as a lever for the final emancipation of the working class, that is to say, the ultimate abolition of the wages system [i.e. capitalism].

In his famous pamphlet, *What is to be Done*, written in March 1902, Lenin directed his chief attacks against those whom he called 'economists', i.e. those who sought economic and social improvement for the Russian people and not the revolutionary overthrow of the system that was his objective. In his polemic, Lenin wrote:[16]

We must bear in mind that the struggle with the government for partial demands, the winning of partial concessions, are only petty skirmishes with the enemy, petty encounters on the outposts, whereas the decisive engagement is still to come.

This is the theoretical basis from which spring many of the wild-cat and unofficial strikes, the efforts made by the Marxists to persuade rank-and-file members not to accept agreements (or maintain them) even when they have been negotiated by their own union. It is the basis for both violent picketing and not only the physical attacks on the police, but their denigration as 'fuzz', 'pigs', etc., i.e. as the defenders of the bourgeois state. It is truly the unity of theory and practice being brought into the service of heightening 'class consciousness'.

In Britain, in particular, because of the historical evolution of the Labour Party and that party's dependence on the unions, Marxists regard the unions as having a special role to play. In 1952 the British Communist Party adopted its programme for the achievement of power in Britain, 'The British Road to Socialism', and at the Congress its then leader, Harry Pollitt, laid down the guidelines when he said:[17]

In the factories and other places of work, workers of all political opinions confront the employing class in defence of their common interests. Here the activity of Communists, in close association with the Labour members and others, has to be directed to strengthening the fighting spirit and solidarity of the workers in the struggle to defend and advance the wages and conditions of every section of workers.

It also means bringing to our fellow workers the class outlook that only Communists can give, by political education that links the struggles in factories against the war policy of the Tories and shows the need to end capitalist rule and replace it with a people's democracy.

Since then, despite minor amendments, the same tactical line has been pursued. What is of immediate significance is the advice that Pollitt gave concerning the penetration of the Labour Party although that has possibly been more successfully achieved by Trotskyists and Maoists than by orthodox Communists. The guidance that Pollitt gave was:[18]

The struggle in the factories will be reflected in the trade union branches, which will more and more express the growing militant unity and class outlook of their members in the factories. The trade union branches in turn will express it in the election of officials and of delegates to their union conferences, of delegates to Labour Parties and trades councils, and the nomination and selection of candidates for local and parliamentary elections. Communists should everywhere be working with the Labour Party and non-Party members of their trade unions branches, in order to help them in choosing for these positions the most militant and class-conscious members of the branch, and in putting forward a working-class policy on all issues, as opposed to the collaboration policy of the right-wing trade union and Labour leaders.

The members of our Party should be working with members of the Labour Party to ensure that their trade union branches are affiliated to their local Labour Parties, that militant delegates are sent and attend regularly, and that those delegates are mandated on all important issues.

The present attack on the so-called right-wing Labour and Trade Union leaders, is reminiscent of the Comintern characterization of non-Marxists as 'Social Fascists' in the 1920s and 1930s, and underlines the importance of another point Pollitt made in his report when he laid it down that:

It is high time that the rank and file of the trade union movement forced their leaders either to change their present reactionary policies, or get rid of them to make way for leaders who know what the true functions of trade unionism are, and will guarantee that they are carried out.

Faced with the evidence of Marxist theory, practice and intention it is necessary to ask how freedom can be defended. Too few of those who would claim to be Liberal Democrats have asked themselves what will be the fate of Britain by the year 2000. Even where the nature of the battle has been comprehended it has seldom been joined. Britain is confronted with the challenge of growing violence, increasing industrial conflict, a further weakening of traditional morals and values, and mounting cries for the escalation of class conflict. The challenge has to be taken up.

The challenge is to build a society which combines freedom, enterprise and incentive with social compassion. The cry of *vae victis* should ring in our ears. If Liberal Democracy should fall, no return match would be permitted by the type of régime which would replace it. Thus its defence is the most important political and educational task for the last quarter of this century.

1 Karl Marx: *Selected Works*, Vol. 1, Foreign Languages Publishing House, Moscow 1964, p. 12
2 Ibid. p. 45
3 Pravda Articles, *Soviet News*, London 1950, p. 74
4 *Peking Review*, 23 December 1966, p. 7
5 The *Pyongyang Times*, 15 April 1973
6 Michael Harrington: *The Twilight of Capitalism—A Marxian Epitaph*, Simon and Schuster, New York 1976, p. 28
7 *Short History of the Communist Party of the Soviet Union (Bolsheviks)*. Authorized English translation published in the USSR in 1939, p. 196
8 V. I. Lenin: *One Step Forward, Two Steps Back* (1904), currently available in the edition published by the Foreign Languages Publishing House, Moscow. See also, for commentary, chapter 2 of *Short History of the Communist Party (Bolsheviks)*
9 Marx and Engels: *The German Ideology*, Lawrence and Wishart 1938, p. 69
10 M. I. Kalinin: *On Communist Education*, Foreign Languages Publishing House, Moscow 1949, p. 126
11 A. A. Zhdanov: *On Literature, Music and Philosophy*, Lawrence and Wishart 1950, p. 35
12 Mao Tse-tung: *Selected Works*, Vol. 3, Foreign Languages Press, Peking, p. 70
13 *The Attack on Higher Education* published by the Institute for the Study of Conflict, London September 1977
14 Frederick Engels: *Conditions of the Working Class in England* (1844), Allen and Unwin, London 1943, p. 224
15 Karl Marx: *Value, Price and Profit*, Allen and Unwin, London 1935, p. 94
16 *Short History of the Communist Party of the Soviet Union (Bolsheviks)*, Moscow 1943, pp. 31–9
17 H. Pollitt: *Britain Arise*, Communist Party 1952, p. 22ff
18 Ibid.

Robert Moss

The Defence of Freedom

If we are to succeed in the great struggle of ideas that is under way, we must first of all know what we believe.

F. A. HAYEK: *The Constitution of Liberty* (London 1960)

Every successful revolutionary, like every victorious general, has heeded the advice of the Chinese sage, Sun Tzu, who taught that 'those skilled in war conquer an enemy who is easily conquered.'[1] Trotsky observed that the triumph of the Bolsheviks in 1917 was that of a strong man striking a paralytic.

In the conflict that is sharpening within British society, the power of the forces that are invading our liberties resides less in their innate strength than in the weakness and confusion of those who should be manning the parapets. We are engaged in a battle of ideas, in which the left is seeking to impose a totalitarian conception of society. Effective resistance can only be based on an alternative philosophy—the philosophy of freedom—and a strategy for turning it into practical politics. The weakest point in our defences is that many 'practical' politicians (and businessmen) are either indifferent to ideas—and therefore unsure of what they are defending, beyond their immediate self-interest—or reluctant to do what they know to be right when they fear that this will offend the floating voter or mighty vested interests like the trade unions.

There is no power, as they say, like the power of an idea whose time has come. Or come again, since the most superficial reading of history shows that mankind undergoes long periods of intellectual and spiritual hibernation, when the accumulated knowledge and the most profound moral insights of previous generations go disregarded—or even proscribed as the work of 'obscene and filthy devils', as St Augustine cordially referred to the Greek philosophers. In the fifth century BC educated man knew that the earth was a spherical object, spinning around on its own axis; a thousand years later they thought it was a flat disc.[2]

The idea whose time has come again is freedom. The perennial problem of politics is to determine the proper relationship between the citizen and the government. The twentieth century has so far been dominated by collectivist ideologies—by Marxism and Fascism—that justify an all-powerful State in the name of principles (like absolute equality, or 'social justice' or the need for *lebensraum*) that are supposedly 'higher' than the freedom of the individual and the family. While most of the world is governed by dictatorships of one sort or another, collectivism is profoundly entrenched in the few once-liberal democracies that remain, especially Britain.

Yet most of the modern achievements of Western civilization have been founded on a sense of the unique importance of the individual and the family, a sense that is rooted in the Christian faith. Every society has to strike its own balance between liberty and authority, between the rights of the individual to make his own choices and the need to impose limits on the innate folly and potential for anarchy of fallen man, and between the individual's pursuit of self-interest and his duty to the community as a whole. Freedom is meaningless without responsibility. Edmund Burke spoke of a 'manly, moral, regulated liberty', and his writings represent the most creative fusion, in the Anglo-Saxon tradition, of the rights of the individual and the claims of society and religion.

One of the ideas that is central in Burke is that a healthy society depends on the diffusion of power: that between the citizen and the central government should stand the 'little battalions' —of family, parish, profession, local community —through which he assumes his social identity. Sweep those away, place men at the mercy of a centralized bureaucracy directed by an ideologically committed élite who see the country 'as a *carte blanche* on which they may scribble what they please' and you will end up, according to Burke, with a society fit only for slaves and tyrants.

Burke was contemptuous of those who discourse in the abstract about liberty, because

. . . the circumstances are what render every civil and political scheme beneficial or noxious to mankind . . . Is it because liberty in the abstract may be classed amongst the blessings of mankind, that I am seriously to felicitate a madman, who has escaped from the protecting restraint and wholesome darkness of his cell, on his restoration to the enjoyment of light and liberty?[3]

He also had a salutary scepticism about the capacity of any individual—or entire generation—to approach any understanding of the desirable arrangement of society without the guidance of custom and tradition. This intellectual humility and profound adherence to *continuity* is characteristic of conservatives everywhere. What is not so often perceived is that it is also a basic requirement for the preservation of a society that is open to experiment but immune to revolutionary upheavals.

Economic freedom, is decried by Fascists of 'left' and 'right'; 'When you say liberalism,' wrote Mussolini, 'you say the individual; when you say fascism, you say the state.'[4] The attitude of British Socialists towards economic freedom is succinctly, if inelegantly, summarized by the button sported by Trotskyite demonstrators: 'I don't want a bigger slice of the cake; I want the bloody bakery.' Yet in Britain, more than any other country, the value of economic freedom should be remembered at a time when it is being strangled. The connection between economic pluralism and political pluralism is obvious from Britain's nineteenth-century history; so is the role of the private sector as the most efficient engine of economic progress and higher living standards.

The nineteenth-century consensus in Britain was that the less the State interfered with the way that people conducted their lawful business, the better. Adam Smith had suggested that the role of the government in society should be confined to three basic functions: the defence of the country against foreign invaders; the protection of its citizens against oppression and injustice from fellow-citizens; and the maintenance of public services 'which it can never be for the interest of any individual or small group of individuals to erect and maintain.' Smith's advice was largely followed, with the notable result that government spending—expressed as a percentage of the Gross National Product in constant prices—*declined* from 24% of the GNP in 1800 to only 15% of the GNP in 1900.[5] This was the age when Britain overshadowed the world as a manufacturing and trading nation—and as an imperial power.

In the age of Britain's decline into economic obsolescence and military impotence, the consensus about the role of government in society has radically altered. It is no longer accepted that people know best, and that if they are left to get on with their jobs the country will be both richer and freer. Gone is the Gladstonian maxim, 'it is a rule of finance that governments should reduce their expenditures'. Instead, it is widely accepted—at least until very recently, when the tax demands of an overblown bureaucracy have begun to burden even the lowest-paid workers—that increased 'public' spending is, in itself, a good thing. Constant pressures for more and more government spending have been exerted since 1945, producing a situation in which public spending, as a percentage of the GNP, is higher than 60%.

Those pressures include the temptation for any major party in a parliamentary democracy to treat elections as auctions, offering bribes to special interest groups like public sector employees (who now total seven million) or people receiving welfare payments (a further nine million). They also include the misguided attempts by recent governments to bankroll their way out of recession and to buy wage restraint from the unions by still more spending on nationalized industries and social programmes.[6]

Increased public spending is the best index of the way that the government has encroached on the people's right to choose. The most stultifying elements in the postwar consensus in Britain have been, first, the belief that the primary role of government should be to promote social justice and equality, and, second, that the government always knows best. It has been accepted, for example, that the welfare of poorer citizens is best secured if the government takes money from the taxpayer in order to spend it on social security (regardless of whether the public is satisfied with it) instead of giving money to disadvantaged citizens and leaving them to decide how to spend it.

The ruling superstition of postwar British politics is the myth of social justice. How many non-Socialist politicians would dare to say that they do not believe in social justice? How many votes would they stand to lose if they said so at election time? Yet, for the reasons set out systematically by Professor F. A. Hayek, the most profound contemporary exponent of the principles of a free society, the concept of social justice is 'the gravest threat to most other values of a true civilisation.'[7]

Why? Because to demand 'social justice' is to make out that 'society' is responsible for relative differences in wealth and living standards that stem from differences in native ability and initiative, and that 'society' should iron them out. Since 'society' is not some great disembodied being, what this boils down to in practice is the demand that the government should play the part of the leveller. In Britain, higher incomes are virtually confiscated by the government and high earners driven into exile, on the grounds that it is 'unjust' that some people should earn noticeably more than others. There is a campaign to abolish grammar schools and hospital pay beds, on the grounds that it is 'unjust' that some families should have opportunities that are not open to others—no matter what sacrifices they have to make to achieve them.

As Hayek observes, the demand for social justice is part of 'an ideology born out of the desire to achieve complete control over the social order, and the belief that it is in our power to determine every aspect of the social order.'[8]

Britain has not reached the stage of collectivist control where the State sets out to determine everyone's conditions of life in every detail. But this is the ultimate logic of an attempt to pursue the concept of 'social justice' all the way. Under a newly-established Marxist régime in Mozambique they have already taken to issuing edicts on the maximum thickness that is permitted for the soles (and heels) of shoes for people of different ages and sexes.

A free society allows the individual to reap the rewards of success in his own efforts, and to run the risks of failure. If you say that the individual is *not* responsible for his own failure and that 'society' owes him a 'just' standard of living regardless of effort, you will destroy the incentive to work and produce, as we have become bitterly aware through the workings of the welfare state in Britain. But you also will destroy something infinitely more precious: the whole basis of traditional morality and the family. The reason is simple. If you tell parents that it is not their duty, but that of 'society' to feed their children, ensure their education and plan for their future, you remove the basic cement of family life. The end product is a degenerate species, that of Welfare Man, or *homo gratificator*, who believes that it is only 'just' that society should supply his every want, and maybe even cater to his fantasies as well.

The idea that the role of government is to impose social justice has contributed to the derangement of the State in modern Britain. While government is weak in areas where by tradition it should be strongest, like defence, it is overmighty in areas which it should never have entered, as in the case of many of the nationalized industries. The defence of freedom in British society will depend on restoring the balance between the State and the individual. In practical terms, this will require radical cuts in taxation and in the overall level of government expenditure. It will involve a strategy for denationalization of State-run industries, and for the revoking of the statutory monopolies that allow notoriously inefficient corporations like the post office to put up prices as they choose in order to subsidize overmanning.

Above all, it would involve a fundamental reform of the welfare state, based on the principle that governments concerned with providing a safety net for the weakest and poorest members of society should subsidize people, not things. The simplest way to achieve this is through a negative income tax that would provide people below the poverty line with the money to maintain their living standards and to purchase basic services. Apologists for the welfare state often talk as if the only way to ensure that low-income families have adequate schooling, health services and housing is for the public sector to provide them. This simply does not follow, but is a typical example of the reactionary character of Socialism in the Britain of the 1970s.

It is entirely possible to reconcile freedom of choice with the provision of the social safety net through negative income tax or through other devices like the voucher scheme for education, which would enable parents to choose the school—whether private or State-controlled—which they consider most appropriate for their children. This, in very simple outline, could be the basis for a radical shift from collectivism to freedom of choice. The fact that it has not been seriously considered by past Conservative governments, which have tended to take only a half-step backwards from the five or six steps forward into State control that had been taken by previous Labour governments, is a symptom of the inevitability complex that is at the heart of postwar consensus politics. This amounts to the assumption that history is a linear progression towards bigger government, more comprehensive social services, higher taxation, and ever-greater interference with the way that people run their lives—all in the name of equality and social justice.

For Socialists, this process is not only inevitable, but right, since for them it is an article of faith that differences of earnings, education and life-style should progressively be eliminated. However much they may dislike the process, many non-Socialists have tended to accept that, at best, it could be slowed down, not halted. This is especially true of those who are unsure of their own philosophy, nagged by doubts about the morality of the capitalist system. So the British political debate for much of the postwar period has revolved around the speed, not the direction, of the march towards what I have described elsewhere as Anglocommunism.[9]

If the consensus has begun to be seriously challenged, it is partly because many ordinary people are suffering from a repressive tax system. Britain has reached the point where wage earners who receive supplementary benefits because their family income is below the poverty level are having to pay taxes. It has been calculated that two-thirds of the workforce pay more in taxes than they receive back in social benefits, however generously that term is defined. Given the choice, it is evident that a large majority of tax-payers would prefer to scrap the present system of social services and receive back in tax rebates the percentage of their income that is presently mulcted to enable them to enjoy the benefits of a national health service and a comprehensive school system that are coming apart at the seams.

But the inevitability complex is built upon fear as well as false assumptions, and above all, fear of the trade unions. Even more urgent than the need to restore the balance between the State and the individual is the necessity to return the trade unions to their basic and indispensable role as representatives of the interests of their members and to discourage their leaders from attempting to operate as an unelected government. Dr Stephen Haseler has written elsewhere[10] about the danger of Britain evolving into a 'TUC one-party state'. Trade unionism is only compatible with a free society in certain conditions, which may be briefly described as follows:

1   If trade unions exercise the same rights and responsibilities as other groups and individuals under the common law of the land
2   If the rights of employees to belong or not to belong to unions are fully and equally guaranteed
3   If strike action is subject to an agreed procedure and legal protection against intimidatory tactics and is not permitted to jeopardize public safety
4   If there are guarantees for ordinary democracy within trade unions, so that their leaders are genuinely representative of the membership[11]

None of these conditions applies in Britain today, where non-union members are increasingly in the position of second-class citizens and where union members themselves have little or no influence over the conduct of officials elected (or appointed for life, like Clive Jenkins of ASTMS) by a small percentage of those entitled to vote in union ballots. The closed-shop legislation brought in under the Labour government in 1974 is an affront to individual liberty, unparalled elsewhere in Western Europe, that probably contravenes the European Declaration of Human Rights. The present legal position is that a man can be sacked for refusing to join a union under a closed-shop arrangement unless he becomes a convert to some obscure religious sect whose statutes specifically outlaw union membership—and even then, he will have to endure the humiliation of producing co-religionists to bear witness to his faith. This has been allowed to happen in a society in which a majority of the workforce is still non-unionized. And this repressive legislation has been swallowed, with barely a hiccup, by the Conservative spokesmen on industrial relations—although, at the time of writing, there are signs of a change of heart in that quarter.

If it is truly impossible, as is sometimes suggested, to govern Britain against the wishes of an unrepresentative clique of union leaders, then Britain has already ceased to be a Parliamentary Democracy, and real power resides in Congress House, not the Palace of Westminster. I do not believe, however, that this is yet the case. To begin with, it is increasingly apparent to most people in Britain that trade unions today are no longer fighting for the same cause as the Tolpuddle Martyrs. Far from defending downtrodden workers who are forbidden to combine, they are seen to be championing the sectional selfishness of an aristocracy of better-paid workers—who are able to be paid more than the market allows, by diverting resources from other areas and so contributing to unemployment—and to be operating as press-gangs that oblige unwilling employees to send an annual subscription to maintain the lifestyles and strike funds of the union leadership.

The image of British trade unionism was hardly enhanced by the violent scenes outside Grunwick in July, when rent-a-mob pickets from as far afield as Scotland, Northern Ireland and Yorkshire were brought into North West London in the effort to coerce the management and staff of a small, efficient company into recognizing a union that the workforce do not wish to join. 'If we cannot crack Grunwick, we cannot crack anything,' said Tom Jackson, the chief of the Union of Postal Workers, early in the dispute. The pluck of this small company, and above all, of the Asian women employees who braved hordes of Marxist rowdies screaming obscenities to go to work on their bus every morning, exposed the unacceptable face of British trade unionism.

How many rank-and-file trade unionists really feel proud of the spectacle of a major union paying its members £15 a day plus £5 for lunch (which is what the National Union of Mineworkers paid the rent-a-mob pickets who turned up at Grunwick) to join politically inspired disputes that have nothing to do with them? The moment is ripe for a new attempt to reconcile the claims of the trade unions with those of the community as a whole. It should involve the repeal of closed-shop legislation; adequate constraints on the right to picket to prevent intimidation; new legislation to restrict the disruption of services vital to public health and safety, like water, gas and electricity; and provision for the democratic (and regular) election of union officials through the secret postal ballot, which should be made compulsory.

I have written of restoring the balance between the individual and the State, and society and the unions. But there is an equally urgent need to redress another kind of imbalance: between the rule of law and the power of transient majorities in Parliament to issue *diktats* in the guise of legislation, which led Lord Hailsham to describe our present political system as an 'elective dictatorship'.[12] The survival of freedom depends on the recognition of an 'assured private sphere'[13]—an area into which governments will not intrude—and on the recognition of universal laws to which all men are subject.

A situation in which a single parliamentary assembly can make and unmake laws with a majority of one vote (and no quorum), without respect for custom, common law, or public opinion on any given issue, is perilous for freedom. It must be remedied by the constitutional definition—through a new Bill of Rights with entrenched clauses—of those basic rights and liberties which need to be protected against trespass by governments. This should involve the creation of a supreme court to rule on the constitutionality or otherwise of what governments propose to do.[14] The National Association for Freedom's fifteen-point Charter of Rights and Liberties may serve as a thumbnail sketch of this new Bill of Rights:

1   The Right to be defended against the country's enemies
2   The Right to live under the Queen's peace
3   Freedom of movement within the country and in leaving or re-entering it
4   Freedom of religion and worship
5   Freedom of speech and publication
6   Freedom of assembly and association for a lawful purpose
7   Freedom to withdraw one's labour, other than contrary to public safety
8   Freedom to belong or not to belong to a trade union or employer's association
9   The Right to private ownership
10 The Right to dispose or convey property by deed or will
11 Freedom to exercise choice or personal priority in spending, and from oppressive, unnecessary or confiscatory taxation
12 Freedom from all coercive monopolies
13 Freedom to engage in private enterprise and pursue the trade or profession of one's choice without harassment
14 Freedom of choice in the use of State and private services (including education and medicine)
15 The Right to protection from invasion of privacy

This seems to me to be a fairly complete list of the rights enjoyed by the citizen within a free society. Many are clearly not regarded as rights at all by British Socialists. The Labour Party, for example, is formally committed to the 'common ownership of the means of production, distribution and exchange'. If seriously applied, this formula would suspend six of the basic rights (9–14) set out in the Association's Charter. It has already produced a plan for the State takeover of the clearing banks.

Finally, there is the need for Britain to make a greater contribution to maintaining the strategic balance between NATO and the Soviet bloc. In a previous essay, Winston Churchill MP has given the measure of Britain's decline as a military power, a process which a Labour Party committee chaired by Ian Mikardo would like to hasten by the scrapping of the Polaris submarine and a further 28% cutback in the overall level of defence spending.

But the international conflict must not be viewed in purely military terms. There are other challenges to world peace, including a population explosion that, on present trends, will increase the total world population to seven billion by the end of the century, and to fourteen billion by the year 2035. There is also the *internal* challenge from Soviet-sponsored subversion.

The Soviet Union—which is the *only* foreign power that poses a strategic threat to Britain—is promoting internal conflict and subversion throughout Western societies, and the recent writings of Boris Ponomarev and less prominent Soviet ideologues provide a blueprint for the Marxist takeover of democratic countries through the destruction of the private sector, the censorship of the media, and the infiltration (or neutralization) of the police and armed forces.[15] This broad Soviet strategy is accompanied by a campaign by the KGB's Disinformation Department (Department 'A' of the First Chief Directorate) to discredit those institutions and political leaders in Western countries that are seen to pose effective opposition to Communist ambition.

So far, I have been mainly writing about measures that should be taken by *government*, like the selling-off of Cable and Wireless, a new law on picketing or a policy of rearmament to cope with a situation in which there is abundant evidence to suggest that the Russians are bent on strategic dominance in order to impose their political will on Western Europe.[16] They add up to a programme for the systematic defence of our freedoms that goes some distance beyond what any British political party has so far been ready to pledge.

But the defence of freedom is too important to be left to professional politicians. Every Marxist knows that the battle of ideas is to be fought out at every level of our society—on the factory floor and in the schools, in broadcasting studios and civil service unions. Jean-Paul Sartre declared that Marxism, as a system of ideas, is 'unsurpassable in our times'. In an intellectual sense, he has already been proved wrong, by the failure of Marxist prophecies about how the capitalist system would break down in advanced industrial societies. Yet the slogans of Marxism (whether or not they are recognized as such) retain an incantatory appeal and form the basis for what the French social philosopher, Raymond Aron, has characterized as a new 'vulgate'—a body of simplified statements of dogma that are accepted on faith and colour the language, and hence the thought-processes, of contemporary political discussion.[17] Its spell is so binding that non-Socialist politicians have often given the impression of men 'caught up in another man's dream', as Lord Coleraine stingingly described those of his colleagues who welcomed the 'Butskellite' consensus of the 1950s.[18]

Release from the spell will hinge on the determined propagation of an alternative system of values—of the virtues of an open society that cherishes individual effort, as opposed to a closed society where the state controls everything. We do not have to wait for the emergence of some prophet of the post-Marxist era to undertake this task. What is required is the return to the great tradition of British pluralism. The Argentine novelist, Borges, once wrote a fantastical tale of a man who sat down and re-wrote *Don Quixote* line by line in longhand, and found he had written a new book.[19] The moral of the story was that the rediscovery by each person of pre-existing ideas is always a new and creative experience.

It is a totalitarian instinct, by contrast, to wish to tear down the past and fashion a new society out of new bricks—an instinct that was given its definitive expression by Rousseau, who wrote:

> . . . he who dares to undertake the making of the people's institutions ought to feel himself capable of changing human nature, of transforming each individual, of altering man's constitution for the purpose of strengthening it.[20]

Social revolution always involves terror, because the social revolutionary wishes to rearrange the human mind, as well as existing institutions. Robespierre speaks for the Jacobin instinct throughout history:

> . . . the basis of popular government in time of revolution is virtue and terror: virtue without which terror is murderous, terror without which virtue is powerless.[21]

He is echoed, ominously, in recent statements from the British left, including statements from Labour MPs.

The lengths to which the totalitarians who are operating inside the British Labour movement are prepared to go where revealed in one of the most extraordinary social documents of 1977. This was an article published in the Communist newspaper, the *Morning Star*, on 29 June. It was signed by Sydney Bidwell, a leading left-wing Labour MP and a past chairman of the Tribune Group. There was nothing unusual about his choice of an outlet; many Labour MPs write for the Communist press, and this is symptomatic of the fact that the Labour Party contains a strong Marxist faction that would no doubt sign up with the Communist Party in a country like France or Italy, where Communists get elected to Parliament.

What was striking was Mr Bidwell's candour, both about the degree of convergence between the Labour left and the Communists, and about the weapons that the left is prepared to use in the effort to establish a form of 'Anglocommunism'. Bidwell observed that his differences with the Communist Party are 'negligible'. It seems that he parts company with the Communists on only one substantive issue. While the Communists' draft policy document 'The British Road to Socialism' says that it is possible to communize Britain without bloodshed, Mr Bidwell is not so sure. 'I wish to be less categorical,' he says. In his view, it may not be possible to achieve genuine Socialism without civil war, since 'counter-revolutionaries' have a nasty habit of resisting attempts to consign them to the scrap-heap of history. Hence revolutionary violence may be unavoidable on the road to 'people's power'.

To employ a phrase beloved of James Joyce, the Bidwell article was a kind of *epiphany*, a 'showing-forth' of one of the maladies that besets the British body politic. Mr Bidwell is a man *in* Parliament, not a man *of* Parliament. Like any good Leninist, he will make use of the democratic system so long as it serves his purpose. But it is the end—which appears to be a variety of Socialism a shade or two redder than the system sketched out in that relatively modest document, the *Communist Manifesto* of 1848—that is all-important. Mr Bidwell is prepared to endure civil war in order to achieve that end, so he is presumably unlikely to have many qualms if 'bourgeois' free-doms (like the freedom of the press) have to be abolished in order to establish 'true Socialism'.

Mr Callaghan tried to shunt the incident aside with a joke when Mrs Thatcher brought it up in the House of Commons. She might have observed that there is no one on the 'Right' of that assembly who talks the way that Mr Bidwell does. It is diffi-cult to imagine a prominent Conservative backbencher writing an article for *Spearhead*, the organ of the National Front, suggesting that 'genuine Fascism' (or some euphemism for it) is desirable, even at the cost of civil war. The totalitarian temp-tation is characteristic of the left in British politics rather than the right.

Mr Bidwell's views might be compared with those of the aspir-ing Jacobins of *Socialist Worker*, which commented, in the midst of the Grunwick dispute, that this episode had provided further proof that there was 'no parliamentary road to Socialism' in Britain, and that a 'workers' militia' should be set up as a step towards the creation of a 'dictatorship of the proletariat'.[22] The vital distinction, of course, is that no open member of the Social-ist Workers' Party, the Communist Party, or any other explicitly Marxist-Leninist Party has a seat in the House of Commons. Sydney Bidwell does.

I doubt whether many of his colleagues on the Labour benches can have welcomed his outburst in the *Morning Star*. Those who share his views must worry that such frankness tends to give the game away. But there are probably still many Clause IV Social-ists who honestly imagine that their purposes are compatible with a real measure of personal freedom and representative government, and even (strangest of all) that they are offering what the British people want.

Yet the previous contributors to this book have explained how Socialism inevitably means more government and less choice. The growing power of central government and the trade unions has eroded individual and economic freedom, deterred private investment, and produced a deepening social and intellectual revolt. What can be read between the lines in Mr Bidwell's article is an angry admission that the British people will not put up with it for ever. He has done us a great service by showing the lengths of which doctrinaire left is prepared to go if the people in Britain should call for the restoration of their freedoms and if a government is elected which is prepared to respond to them.

Is a people that has contributed so greatly to freedom really going to allow the totalitarians to have their way? I cannot believe that it will. But it is late in the day, and the totalitarian left has won positions of influence that it will not quietly vacate. An inevitable confrontation is looming up, between those who wish to uphold (and restore) freedom and those who wish to complete the forced march to the concentration camp society called Socialism.

It is a struggle that transcends the familiar party divides, and the artificial distinctions that are drawn between 'right' and 'left'. Its outcome will determine whether Britain will remain a pluralist, Christian society—and possibly also whether it will remain a Parliamentary democracy. It cannot be complacently ignored, or solved by the kind of difference-splitting that results in signing treaties with the invader on the invader's terms. 'Whoever has not felt the danger of our times palpitating under his hand, has not really penetrated to the vitals of destiny, he has merely pricked its surface.'[23] What is now demanded of the British people is another of those creative feats of constitutional and social innovation that once made it the pacemaker of the Western world.

1 Sun Tzu: *The Art of War*, trans. Samuel B. Griffith (New York 1971) p. 87

2 Cf. Arthur Koestler: *The Act of Creation* (London 1964) for further example

3 Edmund Burke: *Reflections on the Revolution in France* (Everyman edition, London 1960) p. 6

4 Benito Mussolini: 'The Doctrine of Fascism' reprinted in Michael Oakeshott (ed): *The Social and Political Doctrines of Contemporary Europe*

(London 1939) p. 177

5   A. T. Peacock and J. Wiseman: *The Growth of Public Expenditure in the United Kingdom* (London 1976)

6   For an excellent analysis, see David Galloway: *The Public Prodigals* (London 1976)

7   F. A. Hayek: *Law, Legislation and Liberty*, Vol. II (London 1976)

8   Ibid.

9   Robert Moss: 'Anglocommunism' in *Commentary* (New York) February 1977

10 *Daily Telegraph*, 7 July 1977

11 For an expanded argument see Robert Moss: *The Collapse of Democracy* (London 1975)

12 *The Listener*, 21 October 1976

13 F. A. Hayek: *The Constitution of Liberty*

14 For some valuable suggestions, see Lord Scarman: *English Law—the New Dimension* (London 1975)

15 The most definitive guide to Ponomarev's department is Leonard Shapiro's article in *International Journal* (Toronto) spring 1977. On Communist takeover tactics, see A. Sobolev's article in *The Working Class and the Contemporary World* (Moscow) No. 2, 1974; Ponomarev's article in *World Marxist Review* (Prague) No. 6, 1974 and 'On the question of the revolutionary process in Chile' by M. F. Kudachkin and V. G. Tkachenko in the Soviet historical journal, *Novaya: Noveishaya Istoriya*, November/December 1976

16 See, most recently, Richard Pipes: 'Why the Soviet Union Thinks it could Fight and win a Nuclear War' in *Commentary*, July 1977

17 Raymond Aron: *Plaidoyer pour l'Europe décadente* (Paris 1977)

18 Lord Coleraine: *For Conservatives Only* (London 1970) p. 118

19 Jorge Luis Borges: 'Pierre Menard, Author of Don Quixote' in *Fictions*, ed. A. Kerrigan (London 1965)

20 Jean-Jacques Rousseau: *The Social Contract*, trans. G. D. H. Cole (New York 1950) p. 38

21 Quoted in Robert R. Palmer: *The Age of Democratic Revolution: The Struggle* (Princeton 1964) p. 35

22 *Socialist Worker*, 2 July 1977

23 José Ortega y Gasset: *The Revolt of the Masses* (New York 1952) p. 21

The Philosophy of Freedom

'But if you w–want to be free, you've g–got to be a p–prisoner. It's the c–condition of freedom— t–true freedom.'

'True freedom!' Anthony repeated in the parody of a clerical voice. 'I always love that kind of argument. The contrary of a thing isn't the contrary; oh dear me, no! It's the thing itself, but as it *truly* is. Ask any die-hard what conservatism is; he'll tell you it's *true* socialism. And the brewer's trade papers: they're full of articles about the beauty of true temperance. Ordinary temperance is just gross refusal to drink; but true temperance, *true* temperance is something much more refined. True temperance is a bottle of claret with each meal and three double whiskies after dinner . . .'

'What's in a name?' Anthony went on. 'The answer is, practically everything, if the name's a good one. Freedom's a marvellous name. That's why you're so anxious to make use of it. You think that, if you call imprisonment true freedom, people will be attracted to the prison. And the worst of it is you're quite right.'

> ALDOUS HUXLEY: *Eyeless in Gaza* (London: Chatto and Windus 1936) pp. 122–3.

For us, for whom 'Freedom is more than a word, more than the base coinage of politicians, the tyrant's dishonoured cheque', it is essential to begin by getting clear about the meaning which we are giving to this key term; and by making in so doing some fundamental distinctions[1]. After that I propose to do the same for the word 'democracy', considering how far democracy itself is or is not in theory and in practice connected with an essential to various liberties. Finally I shall conclude with a few words on why I myself believe that freedoms matter.

Political liberties, what they are and what they are not

Political freedom, though it can be achieved and maintained only by powerful positive measures, is in itself—like peace—essentially negative. 'The free man', wrote the French *philosophe* Helvetius, 'is the man who is not in irons, nor imprisoned in a gaol, nor terrorized like a slave by the fear of punishment'; and, he added, 'it is not lack of freedom not to fly like an eagle or swim like a whale.' A century earlier the Englishman Thomas Hobbes had put it still more tersely: 'A free man is he that . . . is not hindered to do what he hath the will to do.' It is a pity that he did not add that, always supposing that people would in fact intervene to constrain or coerce a person if he were to attempt to do something, then that person must remain in that respect unfree. For this is so even if he happens to have absolutely no wish to do whatever it may be. I do not become free to leave the place in which I have been imprisoned simply by being content to stay where I am.

The semantic crux with political freedom—the crux, that is, about the meaning of the expression 'political freedom'—makes no reference to what the agent is or is not either capable of doing or inclined to do, nor even to what is actually felt to be burdensome or confining. Freedom in this political understanding simply is the absence of coercion or constraint by other people: whether these human obstacles are such as make it physically impossible to follow some course; or whether they consist in sanctions applied to those who take it. Thus the citizen of Soviet Germany (the German Democratic Republic) is not at liberty to move into the German Federal Republic: both because the confining wall has been made as near as can be impenetrable; and because it is a criminal offence to attempt to escape. And all such political restrictions apply equally to the discontented and to the contented.

1 The adjective 'political' is introduced here mainly in order to exclude the freedom of the will. That is something which in a book of this sort—as indeed in human life in general—has to be taken for granted. Discussion of and demand for political freedoms would lose most if not all their point if we

could not assume that at least some human actions and absten-
tions from action could have been, and could be, other than they
were, and will be. That this almost inescapable assumption is in
fact true I have myself tried to show elsewhere.[2] Here it should be
sufficient to bring out that those who reject it become thereby
committed to depreciating political freedom.

In a much-read work of the forties, a work boldly claiming to
express *The Scientific Attitude*, the Cambridge geneticist C. H.
Waddington wrote: 'Freedom is a very troublesome concept for
the scientist to discuss, partly because he is not convinced that, in
the last analysis, there is such a thing.'[3] The implications come
out most clearly in a perhaps even more widely read book of the
seventies. For, under the sinister title *Beyond Freedom and Dignity*, and on the basis of what he sees as a scientifically grounded
rejection of any such freedom of the will, the Harvard psycho-
logist B. F. Skinner again and again pooh-poohs political liberties. For example: Skinner quotes 'A news weekly, discussing the
legal control of abortion'. This journal argued that '"the way to
deal with the problem forthrightly is on terms that permit the individual, guided by conscience and intelligence, to make a choice
unhampered by . . . statutes".'

'Just so', agrees the lover of liberty, 'it should be by law a
woman's right to choose.' But Skinner, believing that science
both presupposes and reveals that really there is no such thing as
choice, responds only with a sneer: 'The individual is "permitted"
(sic) to decide the issue . . . in the sense that he (sic) will act because of consequences to which legal punishment are no longer
to be added.'[4] (Did someone say: 'Male chauvinist pig'?)

2 Next there are people who want to restrict the word
'liberty' to those freedoms which it is thought that we ought to
have; and which, if available, we are either morally required or
entitled to exercise. Thus, in his essay, the *Tenure of Kings and
Magistrates*, the poet and champion of the liberty of unlicensed
printing John Milton wrote: 'None can love freedom but good
men; the rest love not freedom but licence.' At the end of the following century men of quite another stamp, proto-Leninists of the
French Jacobin clubs, used to say: 'No man is free in doing evil.
To prevent him is to set him free.'

Any such usage must be rejected totally. It obscures the vital truth. A liberty which someone ought not to have at all, or which no one, though having, ought to exercise, remains still, like any other liberty, an absence of external coercion or constraint.

3 We also need in the present context to insist upon that qualification 'external'. It is correct English, and often true, to say such things as: 'I was forced to do it, I had promised'; or 'I could not help myself, I felt so ashamed'. But these are constraints of a very different kind from the obstacles put in our way by other people. It is those with which political freedom is directly concerned.

4 This itself must also be distinguished from the promised outcome of any of those programmes of psychological adjustment, or psychological reconstruction, which are sometimes commended as roads to spiritual freedom. It may on occasion be prudent to recognize some actual political constraints as immovable, and to react by redirecting those of our desires to which these constraints constitute an obstacle. But what you do not become, by thus ceasing to want to kick against the pricks, is politically free. Again, there may have been—indeed there was—something magnificent in the deathbed response of the Stoic sage Posidonius. Suffering agonies from disease he insisted, as his philosophy required, that these, like everything else, were expressions of the Cosmic Reason; and therefore welcome: 'Do your worst pain; no matter what you do, you cannot make me hate you.' Yet, whether or not this response is to be accounted a manifestation of the spiritual freedom of Posidonius, political freedom neither is nor can be any kind of recognition of necessity. It is, rather the opening of alternatives; whether these be good or bad, desired or undesired.

5 A much more dangerous and widespread form of confusion consists in accepting that a person is free: not in so far as he 'is not hindered to do what he hath the will to do'; but in as much as he is in fact—perhaps more nilly than willy—developing in some approved and appropriate way. Every such attempt to present some substitute for authentic political freedom as *true* freedom should be seen off in the manner of Anthony in *Eyeless in Gaza*—perhaps in 'the parody of a clerical voice'. The substitutes thus offered may of course sometimes be in themselves good things. Nevertheless always, please, suspect what comes sailing under the false colours of freedom.

The favourite line of argument here is to urge that the real thing is merely negative and formal, whereas the truly worthwhile ideal is, or ought to be, positive and substantial. Worthy but muddled thinkers like Erich Fromm commend true freedom as the spontaneous rational activity of the total integrated personality. Yet, however excellent that ideal, and however necessary a wide range of political freedoms in fact are to its realization, those freedoms themselves cannot simply be equated with any such ideal. The truth is that the concept of political freedom is indeed negative; and, if you like, formal too. In this it is, as has been suggested already, like the concept of peace. Freedom, like peace, is a necessary condition for all manner of other goods which are themselves indisputably positive and substantial.

6   A confusion of an opposite type mistakes liberties to be incompatible with law. For instance: in a generally sympathetic account of the National Association for Freedom (NAFF) Ferdinand Mount writes: '. . . it is an ancient fallacy to imagine that liberty is necessarily linked with order. Both may be highly desirable, but they are distinct from one another.'[5]

They are indeed different. Certainly there can be perfect order and discipline with precious few if any liberties for those subject to it: some countries manage to approach very close to the alleged ideal of Imperial Germany, a society in which everything which is not forbidden is compulsory. Yet that still leaves room for a necessary connection between liberty and law. For, although there can be law without liberty, there can be no liberties without law. My legal liberties are just legal rights created by the machinery of the law—rights which that machinery is supposed to sustain and enforce. When I am granted legal rights within certain spheres to do what I have the will to do, then by the same token the law becomes committed to defending me against unlawful interference. Such legal defence of liberties, is, like all law, at the same time, but in different respects, restrictive. Those laws, for instance, which establish and defend our legal rights to do our own things in our own homes do this by forbidding anyone and everyone to violate those liberties, whether by assault, theft, vandalism or whatever else.

Jeremy Bentham was certainly right to insist that 'Every law is an infraction of liberty'; provided that this is construed to mean only that every law necessarily commands or forbids, with the support of some external sanction. But some laws—not all—establish and defend legal liberties; while without law and order there can, save for those possessed of overwhelming power, be no enjoyment of any liberty at all.

7   Even while dealing with conceptual questions about liberty and freedom I have as often as not employed both words in the plural. This is to take account of the points that we may be free from one thing but not another, enjoy these liberties but not those. Thus, notoriously, the citizens of countries which have achieved freedom from colonial rule may now enjoy fewer legal liberties than they had under the old régime; while equally notoriously, countries of the free world, the world not yet incorporated into Moscow's 'Socialist Commonwealth', may nevertheless be under the lash of other, purely domestic oppressors. The free world, in this understanding, includes all, but not only, those too few countries in which, for instance, a periodical press is free to criticize ministers in office. So the moral is to be ready to ask: 'Freedom from what, precisely what liberties, and for what or whom?'

Notwithstanding that it is nowadays most favoured by spokespersons for various forms of Socialist totalitarianism, the question 'Liberty for what or whom?' is necessary and good. The proper answer is that all citizens should be equal before the law, and hence that all legal liberties must be for all. To this we hear the response of Anatole France; who scoffed at 'the majestic equality of the law that forbids the rich as well as the poor to sleep under bridges, to beg in the streets and to steal bread.'[6] Or perhaps we are told that freedom for a British professor is a very different thing from freedom for the *fellaheen* of Egypt.

Such angry words speak better for the heart than for the head. For in a system under which all are equal before the law, commands will not be directed at the rich or the poor, at the black or the white, but at everyone. Nor are freedoms as such different for those differently circumstanced. The very real and important differences lie, in the one case, between the degrees of temptation to offend against these laws and, in the other, between the abilities to make use of what are nevertheless the same freedoms.

No doubt other contributors will be indicating several of the ways in which even those who are not able or not willing to take advantage of certain freedoms may nevertheless, whether immediately or eventually, benefit from the fact that those freedoms are available also to others; some of whom can, and will. So I will say only two more things under the present head.

First, I for one shall never establish, nor become directly involved in, any competitive business. But it is still possible—let our political economists argue that it is certain—that I and others like me would gain from the removal of all manner of legal restrictions on trade and industry, restrictions which we have no personal inclination to violate. We might, that is to say, almost all of us benefit from a breaking of the State and local government monopolies, from unleashing enterprise and allowing it to win and keep rewards, from permitting investment to be profitable, and so on.[7]

Second, remember Sir Isaiah Berlin's words: 'Everything is what it is: liberty is liberty, not equality or fairness or justice or culture, or human happiness or a quiet conscience.' So, suppose that some of these other things sometimes are, and perhaps even ought to be, bought at the price of less liberty. Then still 'the loss remains, and it is a confusion of values to say that although my "liberal" individual freedom may go by the board, some other kind of freedom—"social" or "economic"—is increased.'[8]

Democracy and liberties

The word 'democracy' is both ambiguous and vague. Yet we cannot do without it or, more importantly, that to which in its primary sense it refers. We need to distinguish three main areas of meaning, approaching the centre from the periphery.

1 The third has, so far as I can see, no essential connection with the political. The big *Oxford English Dictionary* notes, with little enthusiasm: 'In modern use often more vaguely, denoting a social state in which all have equal rights, without hereditary, or arbitrary differences of rank or privilege.' Thus we may describe the social and sporting arrangements of some organization, which is perhaps in working hours hierarchical and authoritarian, as thoroughly democratic: the Managing Director plays football under the captaincy of an apprentice, and so on.

2 With the second we get much warmer. Consider such increasingly common political labels as 'People's Democratic Republic of the Yemen' or 'Somali Democratic Republic'. These are in part to be understood as systematically mendacious window-dressing, designed to deceive the very innocent and those who wish to be deceived. But to show that there is also something else involved, I call two expert witnesses.

The first is the late Abdul Kharume, sometime First Vice-President of Tanzania. He, like his Afro-Shirazi Party in Zanzibar, was strongly influenced by advisers from the self-styled German Democratic Republic. Speaking at the annual convention of the ruling, and of course sole legal party on the Tanzanian mainland, and referring to a recent roundup of the unemployed in Dar-es-Salaam, he said, 'Our government is democratic because it makes its decisions in the interests of, and for the benefit of, the people. I wonder why men who are unemployed are surprised and resentful at the Government . . . sending them back to the land for their own advantage.'[9]

My second witness is Janos Kadar, addressing the Hungarian National Assembly on 11 May 1957, one year after the friendly neighbourhood tanks of imperial 'normalization' had installed him in office: 'The task of the leaders is not to put into effect the wishes and will of the masses. . . . The task of the leaders is to accomplish the interests of the masses. In the recent past we have encountered the phenomenon of certain categories of workers acting against their interests.'[10]

3 In the primary area of meaning, which embraces the only ways in which I am myself prepared to employ the word, it is applied to methods of making group decisions. Where some groups as a whole take decisions by majority vote, it is democratic. So too are those more numerous and important institutions under which decisions are made by delegates, representatives, or other officers who can in due course be voted out.

There are two crucial differences between this sort of sense and that of the previous Section 2. First, that refers only to what those who are allowed to be the people are (by others) supposed to need, or to what it is (by others) thought to be in their interests to have; whereas this gives the last word to them, or us, as the best judges of what they, or we, do actually want—or, at any rate, vote to have. It is almost impossible to exaggerate the practical importance of the two theoretical contrasts indicated so briefly in the previous sentence. For there is a vast world of difference: between, on the one hand, any system which refers ultimately to what you and I and absolutely everybody else— whether wisely or unwisely, whether rightly or wrongly—do actually want; and, on the other hand, any system in which the last word lies with some more or less precisely limited group of activists, or of actual or supposed experts. Such activists and such experts are of their very nature an alien élite (them), labouring to impose upon the rest (us) whatever it may please them to pronounce that we their benighted subjects need—all of course entirely in our best interest!

The principle is exactly the same, although the practice is enormously different, whether the élite is one of Marxist pretended freedom fighters, their power springing from the barrels of their guns and the whips of their security men, or whether it is a social engineering Mafia of former teachers from Essex or from the LSE, all professing Social Democrats happily promoted now to immensely more powerful and—incidentally—much better paid and pensioned Civil Service posts. How fortunate, how very unequally fortunate, these latter are, thus to be able—in the memorable words of Mr Kilroy Silk MP—'to impose their values'; to impose, that is, upon the recalcitrant diversity of our ordinary inexpert humanity their own crushing, mean, bureaucratic ideal of equality, not of opportunity (for all) but of income and outcome (for others).

Again, there is a world of difference: between those for whom the people genuinely means, for better or for worse, everyone; and those for whom only those who have the right—or, more usually nowadays, the left—political opinions really count as the truly deserving people. A vivid illustration of the employment of such a crabbed and privileged concept was provided by the headline under which the pro-Communist Santiago daily, *Puro Chile*, reported election results on 6 March 1973: 'The people: 43%. The reactionaries: 54·7%' Consider, therefore, as a mnemonic slogan: 'Power for the people means power for the people who shout "Power for the people!"'

The second of the two crucial differences between the present and primary sense of the word 'democratic' and that secondary and perverted usage indicated in 2, lies in the emphasis upon actual voting; and in particular upon voting out as opposed to voting in. This last is in today's world of the greatest importance. In the newly created states of formerly British Africa, for instance, most of the original régimes were established as the result of tolerably presentable elections. They may even have continued to retain actual majority support for quite some time. (Much the same could be said about the régime of Adolf Hitler, who once on that account boasted: 'National Socialism is true democracy!') But nearly all of these régimes (like that of Hitler) jettisoned their claims to democratic legitimacy by proceeding in fairly short order to take steps to ensure that it should be impossible—in that good old phrase—'to vote the scoundrels out'.

But if you are committed to democracy as so conceived, then two things follow. First, you cannot and must not allow that any Leninist or other anti-democratic party can become democratic simply by setting itself to achieve power through the instrumentality of elections. Second, you will be able to, and must, deny the democratic legitimacy of any election—however properly conducted—which puts such a party in office. As Lord Attlee once said: 'Democracy is not a one-way street.'[11] For the true democrat the only irreversible must be reversibility.

4 I hope in the not-too-distant future to develop these ideas in a separate article. But the problem now is how and how far is democracy as here understood connected either in theory or in practice with what liberties. A short and general answer is that various freedoms will be necessary if the voters can correctly be said to be freely making decisions as to how to cast their votes. There must, for instance, be effective guarantees against intimidation. It must be possible to get and to spread relevant information, to discuss and to organize. More concretely and particularly, at least the freedoms guaranteed by the published laws of, say, the Czechoslovak Socialist Republic must be realized. (At the time of writing, in February 1977, the signers of Charter 77 were in fact being persecuted there for merely asking that these laws should be enforced.[12]) But these rock-bottom minimum Charter 77 freedoms are still not sufficient. For in Czechoslovakia, as in all other fully Socialist countries, it is illegal for any private person to possess and operate even so modest an instrument of propaganda as a duplicating machine: while it is also illegal to try to organize any group in opposition to that party to which the constitution ascribes 'the leading role'.

It seems, therefore, that some fundamental civil liberties are essential to the concept of democracy; although that is not to say of course that none of these can be or are found in states which are much less than impeccably democratic. But there is also a very strong case for saying that it is in practical fact impossible to combine a fully Socialist economy with democratic politics. If, as I believe, that conclusion is correct then the various other liberties essential to a competitive, pluralist economy are contingently required by—though they do not themselves guarantee—political democracy.[13]

This is a conclusion which I cannot argue here. It must suffice to say two things.[14] First, I construe the word 'Socialist' as it is implicitly defined in Clause IV of the constitution of the Labour Party, and the parallel clause of the constitution of the TUC: a society is Socialist to the extent that 'all the means of production, distribution and exchange', and perhaps the provision of all health, education and welfare services too, are monopolized by the state or other public authorities. Elsewhere and elsewhen this word may have had, or have, quite different meanings. But in Britain today, and for these many years past, to employ it— or to pretend to employ it—in any way substantially different from this, is most wantonly to darken counsel. Second, the most dedicated and formidable contemporary enemies of democracy are in no doubt at all about the practical incompatibility. Thus the Institute of Marxism-Leninism in Moscow recently sketched a programme for achieving total and irremovable power by following 'United Front' or 'Broad Left' tactics:

Having once acquired political power, the working class implements the liquidation of the private ownership of the means of production. . . . As a result, under socialism, there remains no ground for the existence of any opposition parties counter-balancing the Communist Party.[15]

5   Democracy, as the previous Section 4 has indicated, in one way or another presupposes many liberties. But others, which are not essentially and immediately required by democracy as such, may be very widely and drastically curtailed by decisions democratically arrived at, decisions which still maintain the crucial democratic possibility of a future reversal. This obviously applies to Britain today, under the system described by a former Lord Chancellor as 'elective dictatorship'; a system in which the leaders of a party winning less than 40% of the votes cast in the last general election, and hence the votes of less than 30% of all the electors, boast that they have a mandate to force through every single proposal in a packed manifesto.[16] But the possibility would still remain, although it would no doubt be realized much less often, under a different, fairer, and indeed more democratic system: a system, that is, with electoral laws ensuring that no government could attain office without actual majority support; and perhaps providing also that referenda must be held on particular legislative proposals against which some specified large number of electors chooses to petition.

For however fully democratic the system, and however fully everyone is able to and does participate in that system, if an actual majority of the electorate does not want anyone to be free in certain respects, or wants something else more, then decisions can be taken and laws passed which restrict everyone's liberty in that direction, and this without any compensating gain of more liberty for all in some other direction. Today we do in fact meet

many who want to impose a uniform regimen of universal, compulsory—maybe also unstreamed and unsettled—comprehensive
education; and who also want to see legislative steps taken to
abolish all the remaining private schools. That places in these are
available to all but only those few able and willing to pay for
them is seen as intolerable privilege. It is significant that this is
taken as a reason: not for trying to ensure that more people gain
a chance to choose—perhaps by developing an educational
voucher system—but rather for insisting that no one is to have
any choice at all. Such a response shows that the respondents
place little or no value on parental freedom. Suppose that such
people were to achieve a majority. Then we should have occasion
to reflect in words taken from John Stuart Mill's classic essay *On
Liberty*:

The 'people' who exercise the power are not always the same people
with those over whom it is exercised; and the self-government spoken
of is not the government of each by himself, but of each by all the
rest.[17]

Why freedom matters

About this I will say very little, not because freedom is *not* a
fundamental value for me, but because it *is*. It is fundamental
precisely because it is a precondition of everything which is dis-
tinctively human and most worthwhile. It is a precondition, because we cannot in fact, or sometimes in logic, have those other
goods unless we have some appropriate freedoms. Yet it is never
an absolute guarantee, because as beings capable of choice we
can always abuse our opportunities.

So what can I say about this fundamental, and say in general
with reference to a series of particular cases? Consider two great
utterances. The first is one of several supposedly equivalent
formulations of Immanuel Kant's supreme categorical imperative
of morality: 'Act in such a way that you always treat humanity,
whether in your own person or in the person of any other, never
simply as a means, but always at the same time as an end.'[18] The
second is less stilted, and was part of the contribution of Colonel

Rainborough to the Putney Debates of the New Model Army:
'Really I think that the poorest he that is in England has a life to
live as much as the greatest he.'[19]

Here, as so often, he must be allowed to embrace she. It is these
Kantian imperatives—not some infatuated assumption that
egregious wisdom or virtue is resident in the true people—which
command universal suffrage: it is *us* they are governing, and
misgoverning; it is *our* lives which are at stake. It is, again, these
principles which require that all persons should, as far as they
may be able to, develop in their own ways and that laws should
be directed to ensuring that everyone has as much liberty as is
compatible with the equal liberty of others. Finally, and with
reference to that last point, a demonstration that Scripture can
quote the Devil for its own purposes. In one of his too rare epi-
grams Lenin unwittingly summed up the old and true message of
John Stuart Mill, with how much sincerity and understanding I
do not inquire: 'Yes, liberty is precious, so precious that it must
be rationed!'

1   The quotation is, with one small amendment, taken from Cecil Day
    Lewis's poem 'The Nabara'—see, for instance, his *Selected Poems*, Pen-
    guin 1951, pp. 69–85
2   Antony Flew: *A Rational Animal*, Oxford University Press, spring 1978
3   C. H. Waddington: *The Scientific Attitude*, Penguin 1941, p. 110. Com-
    pare F. A. Hayek: *The Road to Serfdom*, Routledge and Kegan Paul
    1944, pp. 143ff and *The Constitution of Liberty*, Routledge and Kegan
    Paul 1960, pp 72ff
4   B. F. Skinner: *Beyond Freedom and Dignity*, Penguin 1973, p. 98. Com-
    pare perhaps my Critical Notice, first published in *Question Six* Pember-
    ton 1973, and reappearing in a revised form in *A Rational Animal*
5   Ferdinand Mount: 'Freedom and the Free Nation' in the *Spectator*, 19
    November 1977, p. 13
6   Anatole France: *Le Lys Rouge*, Paris 1894, p. 117—I borrow this refer-
    ence, with thanks, from F. A. Hayek: op. cit. (1960) p. 493
7   I gladly share the inscription which I copied from a plaque in the central
    marketplace of Singapore in 1969. The words were attributed to Dr Goh

Keng Swee, Minister of Finance, in what curiously claims to be a Socialist government: 'A society for economic growth should nurse the creative talent that its enterprising members possess, and should encourage the development of such talent to its full stature.'

8   Sir Isaiah Berlin: *Four Essays on Liberty*, Oxford University Press 1969, pp. 125–6. Like every friend of freedom I am extensively in his debt

9   I collected this one from the Dar-es-Salaam press the following day—8 July 1967. Although Dar is scarcely one of Ian Fleming's 'exciting cities' I have no difficulty at all in understanding that, and why those who have settled there even into penury, not only do not want to be pushed about 'for their own advantage' but also hate the thought of returning to the, by comparison, excruciating boredom of a Tanzanian village

10 Reported in *East Europe*, July 1957, p. 56. I thank Sidney Hook for this reference from his *Political Power and Personal Freedom*, New York 1962, p. 147

11 Wilfred Sendall: 'Popper: Threats to the Open Society' in M. Ivens (ed.): *Prophets of Freedom and Enterprise*, London, Kogan Page 1975, particularly p. 61

12 A full English translation of Charter 77 is available from the British section of Amnesty International, and a shortened and simplified version was published in *The Free Nation*, 18 November 1977, p. 5

13 It really is not good enough, and suggests bad faith rather than mere stupidity, when leading Labour Party intellectuals try to dismiss what should be a profoundly worrying contention with some slight but quite irrelevant reference to Chile or Brazil—which is all I have myself got from such as I know in my own personal contacts

14 But see, for instance, Milton Friedman: *Capitalism and Freedom*, Chicago University Press 1962, and compare S. Brittan: *Capitalism and the Permissive Society*, Macmillan 1973

15 *The Economist*, 17 June 1972, p. 23. British readers—who must have noticed the threat of drastic and 'irreversible' changes in the 1973 Labour Party *Programme* and the 1974 *Manifestos*, and the development of close party-to-party contacts with the GDR and the USSR seen for instance in the recent visit of Mr Boris Ponomarev—can scarcely help reflecting that the controlling élite does not actually have to be called a Communist Party

16 At the Labour Party Conference in 1974 the then Prime Minister said, 'We have been elected on the policies which we have proclaimed with total clarity in two manifestos within a single year.' His successor chorused: 'The people have now given the Labour Government a clear mandate.'

17 J. S. Mill: *On Liberty*, Everyman edition, p. 67

18 Immanuel Kant: *The Moral Law*, translated by H. J. Paton, Hutchinson 1948, p. 96

19 Quoted in A. D. Lindsay: *The Essentials of Democracy*, Oxford University Press 1929

Milestones in The Constitution and in The Establishment and Curtailment of Rights and Liberties

1086	All property surveyed for taxation purpose by order of William I (1066–1087)
c1180	Possessory assizes established to regulate land disputes. Foundation of English Common Law laid by Henry II (1154–1189)
1215	Magna Carta signed under duress by King John. Four chapters in force today (1978)
1265	The Model Parliament summoned by Simon de Montfort
1284	Wales annexed by Edward I
1327	Keepers (later Justices) of the Peace first appointed
c1350	Parliament became bicameral (two chambers)
1362	English became the language of the Courts
1376	Doctrine of impeachment instituted. Office of Speaker established
1381	The Peasants' Revolt provoked by a poll tax
1395	The House of Commons began to exercise taxation powers
1461	The office of Attorney General (the monarch's lawyer) established
1485	The House of Lords established as the Court of Appeal for civil cases. Position formalized in 1876

170

1495	The Treason Act passed to ensure allegiance to the sovereign
1532	The Court of Session established in Scotland as the supreme civil court
1534	Henry VIII exercised prerogative power to suspend customs. Established himself as head of the Church of England
1535	Privy Council established
1602	Case of Monopolies—the Courts refused to uphold the monarch's grant contrary to statute
1611	Case of Proclamations—the Courts held that the judiciary could determine the limits of the King's prerogative. New offences could no longer be created by proclamation
1616	Chief Justice Coke dismissed by James I for challenging royal prerogative power
1628	The Petition of Right signed by Charles I so limiting his 'divine rights'
1629–1640	Charles I ruled with Parliament dissolved
1637	The Ship Money case upheld the royal prerogative power to tax in time of emergency
1641	The Triennial Act required assemblage of Parliament every three years even if no writs issued by the monarch (reinforced in 1694)
1642–1649	Civil War. Charles I executed on 30 January 1649
1653	Oliver Cromwell assumed title of Lord Protector
1660	The Restoration of Charles II
1662	The Licensing Act censored 'treasonable' tracts and publications. Not renewed after 1695
1665	Taxations by Parliament limited to those designated for specific purposes
1670	Bushell's Case established total privilege in judicial proceedings
1678	Test Act required Anglican oaths for all MPs. Repealed 1828

1679	Habeas Corpus Act forbade imprisonment without prompt trial
1688	The Case of the Seven Bishops established the right to petition the King
1689	Bill of Rights established the relationship between King and Parliament Toleration Act permitted freedom of worship except for Roman Catholics and Unitarians. Modified by Savile's Act in 1778. Catholic MPs permitted after 1829. Under the Coronation Oath Act, the monarch(s) swore to govern according to laws and customs of the realm.
1690	Ireland finally bound to English jurisdiction by defeat of the Catholic James II at the Battle of the Boyne
1695	House of Commons rejected the royal nominee for the Speakership
1701	Act of Settlement established the Protestant succession to the throne
1704	*Ashby* v. *White* established that there should be no right without a remedy
1707	Union of England and Scotland effected Last Royal veto exercised (by Queen Anne) Scottish Militia Bill
1715	Scottish separatists' (Jacobites, named after the self-styled James VIII, the Old Pretender) rebellion put down by the Crown
1716	The Septennial Act provided for the convening of Parliaments for seven years
1717	Royal attendance at Cabinet meetings virtually ceased under George I
1721	Parliamentary questions introduced in the Upper House Sir Robert Walpole became *de facto* the first Prime Minister
1745–1746	The Young Pretender (Bonnie Prince Charlie) defeated at Culloden Moor (1746) so ending pretensions of Stuarts
1760	George III surrendered hereditary royal revenues in return for an annual payment on the Civil List, *ie* payment from funds raised by parliamentary taxation

1763   John Wilkes MP, publisher of the *North Briton Journal,* in-
            directly established freedom of speech and of the press from
            royal libel prosecution

1763–1765   Illegality of general, as opposed to specific, search warrants es-
            tablished by *Leach* v. *Money* and *Entick* v. *Carrington*

1772   Somersett's case proclaimed that slavery was not recognized
            under English Law. Slave Trade abolished 1807

1782   Contractors to HM Government debarred from membership of
            the House of Commons

1783   Office of Leader of the Opposition unofficially established.
            Officially established in 1937

1783   An administration dismissed by the King for the last time

1792   *Grant* v. *Gould* held that order could be restored by the military
            if authorized by the executive

1795   The right of assembly for public meetings restricted

1801   The Irish Parliament ended. The United Kingdom of Great
            Britain and Ireland under a single Parliament (Westminster)

1806   Last impeachment (Lord Melville)

1832   First Reform Act widened male franchise

1833   Judicial Committee of the Privy Council established

1835   Municipal Corporation Act. Borough Council elections provided
            for

1841   Melbourne's resignation set precedent for a dissolution following
            defeat on a major issue

1842   In *Edinburgh & Dalkeith Railway* v. *Wauchope* the Court up-
            held Parliamentary supremacy and curtailed power of the courts
            to inquire into parliamentary deliberation

1843   Lord Chamberlain empowered to censor plays

1844   Lay peers excluded by convention from judicial proceedings of
            the House of Lords

1857	Concept of a public corporation established by Mersey Docks and Harbour Board. Port of London Authority established in 1908
1858	Jews permitted to become MPs. Property qualifications for MPs ended
1866	Comptroller and Auditor General established to monitor governmental expenditure
1867	Walter Bagehot's *The English Constitution* published
1868	Disraeli resigned after General Election defeat
1870	Education Act provided elementary schooling and School Boards
1871	Health legislation administered by Local Government Boards
1872	Secret ballots established
1872	Rural and urban sanitary authorities established
1873	Supreme Court of Judicature Act unified High Court and Court of Appeal
1879	Office of Director of Public Prosecutions established
1881	The Guillotine procedure introduced to curtail parliamentary debate
1883	Electoral expenditure regulated and the Corrupt and Illegal Practices Act passed
1885	A. V. Dicey published his *Introduction to the Study of the Law of the Constitution*
1888	Local Government Act established elected county councils. Extended by a further Local Government Act (1894) to Urban and Rural District Councils and to parish meetings
1901	Taff Vale decision established that a trade union could be sued for damages for the actions of its agents
1905	Office of the Prime Minister first officially recognized
1906	Founding of the Labour Party. Trade Disputes Act permits

'peaceable picketing' of the house of any person in furtherance of a Trade Dispute

1907   Court of Criminal Appeal established with ultimate appeal to the House of Lords

1909   House of Lords rejected the budget leading to the Parliament Act 1911 to end their veto power of money bills

1910   *Amalgamated Society of Railway Servants* v. *Osborne* held that a trade union could not contribute to Members of Parliament and that political levies were illegal

1911   MPs paid salaries for the first time (£400 per annum)

1914   Defence of the Realm Act (DORA) gave Government wide emergency powers in time of war
        War Cabinet (of seven) functioned in lieu of full cabinet Reduced to five in 1916

1915   *Local Government Board* v. *Arlidge* excluded disclosure of documents by a department from rules of natural justice

1918   Franchise extended to all men over twenty-one and to women aged over thirty. Women admitted to membership of the House of Commons

1920   The island of Ireland partitioned into twenty-six southern counties of an Irish Free State and six Ulster counties in the north. The Republic given Dominion status in 1922
        Attorney General v. *De Keyser's Royal Hotel* held that the Crown may not act *ultra vires* of statutory authority

1926   General Strike. Subsequently declared unlawful

1926   British Broadcasting Corporation formed to control wireless transmission. First public demonstration of television in London

1927   Trade Disputes Act declares illegal any strike to coerce Government by inflicting hardship on the public

1928   Franchise extended to all women over twenty-one

1929   Lord Hewart's *The New Despotism* assailed the delegation of legislative power by Parliament to government departments

1931   National (coalition) Government formed

1934   Reaffirmation that Parliament could not bind its successors on future legislation in *Ellen Street Estates Ltd* v. *Minister of Health*

1935   Last trial of a peer by his peers. This privilege abolished in 1948 *Thomas* v. *Sawkins* held that entry into private premises by police lawful if done in belief that an offence was likely to be committed

1936   Public Order Act created the offence of using words or behaviour likely to provoke a breach of the peace

1941   The *Daily Worker* suppressed for several months

1942   *Liversidge* v. *Anderson* upheld a Minister's right to issue a detention order if he claimed 'reasonable cause'
Duncan v. *Cammell Laird & Co* upheld a Minister's right to withhold evidence if he claimed disclosure was contrary to the public (national) interest

1944   Boundary Commissions for England, Scotland, Wales and Northern Ireland established to regularize the size of constituency electorates

1945   Nationalization of coal, steel, gas, electricity, railways, atomic energy, road transport, airlines, docks and the Bank of England

1946   Statutory Instruments Act

1947   Crown Proceedings Act permits the suing of government departments

1948   Plural voting (University and business votes) for parliamentary elections abolished

1948   British Nationality Act
National Health Service established
House of Lords delaying power reduced to one year

1954   Crichel Down affair leads to resignation of the Minister of Agriculture

1957   Attending members of the House of Lords paid daily attendance allowance

1962   Immigration Act imposed restrictions on certain Commonwealth citizens. Further restricted in 1968

1963   Disclaimer of hereditary peerages allowed

1964   Independent Television Authority established by statute

1965   *Burmah Oil Co* v. *Lord Advocate* established right of property owners to compensation for loss caused by government action in time of war. Ruling nullified by War Damage Act, 1965

1965   Capital Punishment abolished

1967   Parliamentary Commission for Administration (Ombudsman) appointed with power to investigate an area of complaints of maladministration

1969   Franchise extended to eighteen to twenty-year-old citizens

1971   United Kingdom adopted a decimal system of currency under which £1 = 100 new pence

1972   Direct rule established by Westminster over Northern Ireland with suspension of the Parliament at Stormont

1972   Prime Minister (Heath) obtains full powers to sign Treaty of Accession to the Treaty of Rome by an innovatory grant of the treaty-making prerogative

1973   United Kingdom joins European Economic Community (Common Market) on January 1 under European Communities Act

1973   *McWhirter* v. *Independent Broadcasting Authority* Intended transmission of T.V. film because deemed 'likely to cause offence' banned by High Court without Attorney General's *fiat*

1976   Clay Cross councillors indemnified by Act from penalties for breaching an Act in Force

1977   House of Lords rules Attorney General is not answerable to the Courts but only to Parliament, which is a part-time body controlled by his own political party

1977   *Gouriet* v. *Union of Postal Workers* Planned strike declared to be a criminal offence despite Attorney General's refusal to grant *fiat*. Attorney General joined as defendant

Contributors' Biographical Notes

Winston Churchill MP

Education: Eton and Christ Church, Oxford. Conservative Member of Parliament for Stretford. 1970–72—Parliamentary Private Secretary to the Minister of Housing. 1972–3—Parliamentary Private Secretary to the Minister of State for Foreign Affairs. 1973—elected Secretary of the Conservative backbench Foreign Affairs Committee, and in 1976 he became Opposition frontbench spokesman on Defence. Author of *First Journey* (1964) and *Six Day War*—the latter with his father the late Randolph Churchill. Council Member of the National Association for Freedom.

Viscount De L'Isle, VC, KG, PC, GCMG, GCVO, MA, FCA, Hon. Fellow Magdalene College, Cambridge, Hon.LL.D. Sydney University

Education: Eton and Magdalene College, Cambridge. Member of Parliament (C) for Chelsea 1944–5. Parliamentary Secretary, Ministry of Pensions 1945. Secretary of State for Air 1951–5. Governor-General of Australia 1961–5. Chairman of Phoenix Assurance Co. Ltd from June 1966. President of the British Heart Foundation from 1976. Founder Member and Chairman of the National Association for Freedom.

Professor Antony Flew, MA (Oxon), D.Litt. (Keele)

Professor of Philosophy, University of Reading. Author of *Hume's Philosophy of Belief* (1961), *An Introduction to Western Philosophy* (1971), *Thinking About Thinking* (1975), *Sociology, Equality and Education* (1976). Vice-President of the Rationalist Press Association and Chairman of the Voluntary Euthanasia Society. Founder Member of the Council of the National Association for Freedom.

178

John Gouriet

Education: Charterhouse School. Former regular army officer. Saw active service in Malaya and Borneo against Communist guerillas. Travelled widely in Asia and Arabia. Staff College operational staff. Merchant banker. Awarded Polish Gold Cross for his part in the Katyn Memorial ceremony. Entered British legal history with his case against the Attorney-General in 1977. Campaign Director of the National Association for Freedom and Member of Council and Management Committee.

Dr Stephen Haseler, B.Sc.(Econ), Ph.D.

Education: London University. Principal lecturer in Politics at the City of London Polytechnic. Author of *The Gaitskellites* and *The Death of British Democracy*. Member of the Greater London Council 1973–7. Chairman of the General Purposes Committee 1973–5. Chairman of the Labour Political Studies Centre from 1972.

Russell Lewis, MA

Education: Caerphilly Grammar School, St John's College, Cambridge. Journalist, Fleet Street. He was Director of the Conservative Political Centre for eight years up to 1975 when he left to write the biography of Margaret Thatcher which reached seventh on the non-fiction best seller list. In January 1977 his report, *The Survival of Capitalism*, was published by the Institute for the Study of Conflict. Council Member of the National Association for Freedom.

Norris McWhirter, MA

Education: Marlborough and Trinity College, Oxford (BA in Economics and International Politics; MA in Contract Law). Author, broadcaster, journalist and athlete. Active service Royal Navy 1943–6. Editor and compiler of the *Guinness Book of Records*. Founder Member and Deputy Chairman of the National Association for Freedom.

Edith, Lady Morrison of Lambeth

Widow of Lord (Herbert) Morrison of Lambeth, CH, was his second wife. Formerly a business executive with great interest in public—particularly social—affairs in her native Lancashire. Her book *Memoirs of a Marriage* (Frederick Muller, 1977) is perhaps the best pen-portrait of the famous Labour statesman, who found in her a great companion and partner during the last ten years of his fascinating political career. Council Member of the National Association for Freedom.

Robert Moss, BA (1st class Hons.), MA

Education: Australian National University. Editor of *Foreign Report, The Economist*'s confidential weekly. Author of *Urban Guerillas, Chile's Marxist Experiment* and *The Collapse of Democracy*. He has also written a number of shorter works including *Revolutionary Changes in Spain* and *Counter Terrorism*. He was the editor of *The Ulster Debate*, and is editor of *The Free Nation*. A regular broadcaster on television and radio. Council Member of the National Association for Freedom and Member of the Management Committee.

Narindar Saroop

Education: Aitchison College, Lahore, and Indian Military Academy. Councillor, Royal Borough of Kensington & Chelsea. Chairman of the Community Relations Committee. Founder and current Chairman of the United Kingdom Anglo-Asian Conservative Society. Prospective Parliamentary candidate for Greenwich. Grandson of Sir Chottu Ram who introduced the very first landed reforms ensuring rights, etc. for tenant farmers. Served as a regular officer in 2nd Royal Lancers (GH). Executive and Director in the City.

Dr K. W. Watkins, B.Sc.(Econ), PhD

Education: Merchant Taylors and London University. Economist and political scientist, teaches at the University of Sheffield. Author of numerous books and articles including *Britain Divided* and *The Practice of Politics and Other Essays*. Founder editor of Nelson's Political Science Library. Editor of 'Men and Movements History Series', Associate Editor (Overseas) of the *Journal of Political and Social Affairs* (Washington). Founder Member of the Council of the National Association for Freedom and Member of the Management Committee.